From
Addiction
To
ADOPTION

ENDORSEMENTS

What people are saying about...

From **Addiction** *To* **ADOPTION**

Need encouragement? Read this book. Rick and Teresa McKinney's lives speak a loud and clear word of hope and encouragement that everyone can relate to. They transparently open their hearts and take you on a journey into the heart of God. As they share their powerful and amazing testimonies, you will be astonished at what the Lord has done. Receive impartation on how to enter your destiny and live an overcoming lifestyle.

> **Ché Ahn**, Senior Pastor, HRock Church, Pasadena, CA; President, Harvest International Ministry; Chancellor, Wagner Leadership Institute

This book is a life-changer in its capacity to offer hope and practical guidance to those who struggle with addictions, whatever they may be. The inspiring testimonies of Rick, Teresa and others, reveal a loving, miracle-working God who will empower us on our journey into freedom and personal transformation.

> **Terry Edwards,** Christian Equippers International

This book is a faith builder and instrument of encouragement. It is a quick and easy read, but also carries a powerful 'punch' in the Spirit! *Real* is the word that comes to me about this book. The McKinneys are real, their personal testimonies are real, and the fruit of their ministry (delivered and set-free souls) is real. Grace & I have ministered with them and have been blessed by a visit as honored guests to the ranch. Reading this book will charge your spirit and enhance your faith in The Lord of Glory!

Pastors Henry & Grace Falany,
Mariposa Revival Center - Mariposa, Ca.
www.MariposaRevivalCenter.com
Author of *"God, Gold & Glory!"*

I have known the McKinneys for more than eleven years. God ordained them to found and lead *New Hope Recovery Ranch*, a ministry expressed by Jeremiah 29:11, "...I give you a future and a hope." Rick and Teresa have exemplified the passage in *I Peter 1:7 "That the genuineness of your faith, being much more precious than gold (that perishes, though it is tested by fire), may be found to praise, honor and glory at the revelation of Jesus Christ."* They stand in HIS grace and walk in HIS truth. (John 1:24) So many lives have been touched with the love of JESUS through this ministry of hope!

Pastor Dallas Ramsey, A Voice in the Wilderness Church

From
Addiction
To
ADOPTION

Set Free To Live
As Favored Children Of God

The Life Journeys Of
Rick & Teresa McKinney
Written by Janet Richards

From Addiction *To ADOPTION*

International Standard Book Number: 978-0-9857450-0-4

From Addiction To ADOPTION was printed in the USA, 1st printing, 2012.

DEDICATION

This book is dedicated to the ones who still suffer "out there" somewhere, and also to those whose hearts are being drawn to help people with addictions. To those who want to help: listen to that pulling on your heart and *JUST DO IT!*

Contents

Changing Lives:
Personal Testimonies From The Ranch

FOREWORD

In Luke 19:10 *(NIV)*, while visiting the house of Zacchaeus, Jesus Christ made the purpose of His mission and ministry perfectly clear in the brief but powerful statement, *"For the Son of Man came to seek and to save what was lost."* In this statement He was referring almost exclusively to the Adamic race, originally created in God's image, but now wrapped in chains of darkness and bondage as a result of sin. In the parable of the lost sheep He reveals His heart for each of us when He challenges His listeners with *"Suppose one of you has a hundred sheep and loses one of them. Does he not leave the ninety-nine in the open country and go after the lost sheep until he finds it (Luke 15:4, NIV)?*

The gospels reveal that there are two primary things that move God's heart. The first is His love for people. The second is His desire for partners. Jesus revealed His heart in Luke 4:18 *(NIV)* when He stood up in the synagogue and quoted from the book of Isaiah what the prophet had prophetically seen of His mission hundreds of years earlier: *"The Spirit of the Lord is on me, because he has anointed me to preach good news to the poor. He has sent me to proclaim freedom for the prisoners and recovery of sight for the blind, to release the oppressed, to proclaim the year of the Lord's favor."* He revealed His desire for partners in calling forth disciples who would continue in His heart and anointing, to carry out His mission after His crucifixion. The apostle Paul describes this mission so well in 2 Corinthians 5:18 *NIV*: *"All this is from God, who reconciled us to Himself through Christ and gave us the ministry of reconciliation."* Those who step into this calling become His partners in glorious, but usually challenging ways.

I have known Rick and Teresa for a number of years and we not only have become good friends, but I have grown to have such a deep admiration for their anointed ministry and their compassionate hearts toward those whom the enemy has bound in life-devastating addictions. Before they knew each other, they each reached out and took the hand of the Good Shepherd, who pulled them out of their own addictions and bondages. After they met and married, the Spirit of God multiplied their faith and compassion, giving them a burden to help those who were bound by similar addictions. This was the beginning of a ministry called **New Hope Recovery Ranch**, which has helped hundreds and hundreds of people over the last decade.

It has not been an easy calling. They started by partnering with Christ in His call and direction, living completely by faith. They embraced a sacrificial vision that would demand that they literally share their lives and their home with men who had hit bottom. They would step into this in their middle-age

12

years, during a time when most people h
future retirement. But true to the heart of
beyond their own comfort to seek and to sa\
lost.

This book is their story as partners with Christ in the ministry
of reconciliation. It is a story of a growing anointing in the
Holy Spirit, to work the works that Jesus worked. It is filled
with inspiring stories of miraculous provision, stories of their
own spiritual growth into deeper revelation and
empowerment, and testimonies of those whose lives were
saved and delivered because of Rick and Teresa's love and
commitment. This story of their journey will bring hope and
keys of breakthrough to those who struggle with addictions
or any of the bondages that work captivity in our lives. It will
stir and inspire all of us to greater partnership with Christ in
His effort to bring salvation, deliverance and restoration to
the lives of others.

Terry Edwards
Pastor, Lake Tahoe Christian Fellowship

INTRODUCTION

I love to write, so of course my curiosity was piqued when, as strangers, Teresa and I happened upon the subject of writing and she invited me to consider shaping their story into book form. We met at their ranch and I listened with fascination to the incredible journey of their lives. Together, we entered into a commitment to work on this project. But it was only later as I sat at the computer and began sorting through the testimonies of their lives, that I felt the Holy Spirit's conviction. Rick and Teresa live a *radical obedience*, with strong faith and courage. Hearing of amazing healings; miraculous provisions; specific and divinely-timed answers; men and women set free from addictions; it slowly dawned on me that the supernatural elements of their lives increased when they risked *everything* to follow God and chase their dreams. Like cowboys swinging into the saddle and heading into the Wild West, the McKinneys' willingness to trust God has opened up realms of answered prayer they could only have experienced by embracing the challenges inherent in adventure.

Rick and Teresa, thank you for your unflinching commitment to follow God. Thank you for complete transparency and humility as you shared your failures, your battles for identity and also your successes. Many have already been inspired through your understandings, and with the unveiling of this book the number of people changed through your lives will only increase. May each person who reads this book be encountered by God in the same way He so powerfully encountered you. Blessings, love and honor from Jesus and from my heart.

Janet Richards
Missionary & partner with her husband, Rusty Richards, in their *Pray Big!* adventure; writer and author of
Unlocking Our Inheritance
http://www.praybig.us

CHANGING LIVES
One At A Time

At *New Hope Recovery Ranch,* there's a heavenly exchange taking place. People are finding their way to our desert haven to trade in worn out, addicted lives that are full of personal devastation and a survivor mentality. In a generous divine 'swap'[1], the Holy Spirit then comes to offer each one His new and hope-filled *life.*

We thought you'd like to hear *God stories* from some of the men and women whose lives have been transformed. You'll find their testimonies highlighted in gray boxes throughout this book, weaving threads of human brokenness into fresh, recreated tapestries of children who are honored and gently led by their heavenly Father.

---

[1] *Colossians 1:13, 14*

We must tell you however, not every person who has come through the doors of the ranch has successfully reentered society to live a great life. A few have left sober, only to come back later in need of another round of detoxification. But, many *have* been set free to return home and rebuild their lives and families, to find good jobs and become part of healthy Christian fellowships. Some have gone on to fulfill dreams of continuing their education. Most serve in some capacity of ministry within the body of Christ. The Spirit of God has restored many lives, raising them from the ashes of destruction and misery.[2] We give honor to Jesus, whose desire for every human being is that they would know heaven's unrelenting love, dignity and honor.

Meet the God of hope in each reclaimed life. Be encouraged and strengthened. Feel His power to change everything. Grow in thankfulness. Enjoy their testimonies!

---

[2] *Isaiah 61:3, 4*

1

DELIVERED INTO SONSHIP
Rick's Story

He wore a uniform, this man whose car mysteriously appeared by the side of the empty desert road where I had laid down to die. "Looks like you need a ride," he offered. Even though all my bodily functions had already shut down in a pre-death state, I managed to crawl through his open car door and we drove fifteen miles without another word.

Somehow, my stranger-chaperone knew to drop me off at the Striper Hotel in Rio Vista, where I was living. I got out of the car near the lobby entrance to head inside and glanced back toward the man to nod my thanks, but he was gone. Seconds after I'd gotten out of the vehicle it had completely vanished, along with its driver. Nowhere to be seen, the angel in human form had materialized on assignment to rescue me from certain death after my first heart attack at age twenty-nine.

Two weeks later I *was* dead. In spite of the angelic deliverance in the desert, I'd returned to my booze like a boomerang. As a hopeless alcoholic I'd failed miserably every time I tried to stop drinking, and when my overloaded heart protested and quit a second time, I found myself standing at the tunnel entrance that leads into heaven. Feeling perfectly sober for the first time in at least a decade, I glanced down at my hands and feet. I was no longer experiencing *Delirium Tremens*, the shaking that accompanies alcohol withdrawal. *This is good!* I thought, *No trembling, no more pain, no fears, no anger, no resentment, nothing negative! I have only complete and amazing peace!*

At the far end of the tunnel, an indescribable brightness roiled in constant movement and beyond it laid a magnificent patch of brilliant blue. Suddenly, as I began walking toward the gleaming white, a figure appeared through the wall of the tunnel and stood in front of me. Silhouetted by the light, the being spoke directly: "You have to go back". I answered emphatically, "I have no intentions of going back!" but he only reiterated, "You must return." I pled and argued, "I'm *not* going back. *Please, please, please* don't make me go back there!"

My body began to withdraw from the tunnel and moments later I awoke in my parents' home. I'd been dead for almost twenty minutes from a second heart attack. Paramedics worked quickly to stabilize my vital signs and we headed for the emergency room with sirens blaring. In a tug of war between life and death, I died again during a third heart attack, but emergency crewmembers in the ambulance brought me back. Finally, I awoke this side of heaven in a sterile ICU room with tubes and needles attached everywhere. Despairing of any hope that I could someday find the strength to slay the giant of my nightmarish drunkenness, I stared up at the institutional ceiling above my hospital bed and wondered why in the world God had insisted I return to planet earth.

Stolen Dreams

Before starting to drink at the young age of eight, I knew and communicated regularly with this God who had preserved my life. My grandmother, made of goodness from the top of her head to the soles of her feet, taught me to talk with Him and through her impartation, He and I became friends.

Hearing His voice was natural in those early years, almost as though God and I were carrying on face-to-face conversations. We could talk about *anything* - my desires to go to Disneyworld, my family's needs - whatever a child thinks about became topics of our discussions. And on most afternoons I could be found sitting in front of our family's television watching healing evangelist, Oral Roberts. Though a young boy, I felt tremendous love for God and for His church, and Oral's anointing stirred great dreams of going into the ministry to become a pastor.

Then one day in the midst of my happiness, I heard an audible voice. The voice said to me, "When you come to a full understanding of all these spiritual things, I'm taking you out. I'm taking you home." Since I hadn't learned there were other beings from the spirit realm that also had the ability to speak, I assumed the voice belonged to God. I thought He was telling me that when I'd learned enough about Him, I would die.

But as a little eight-year old boy, I didn't want to die! From that day on, I made a subconscious decision that God was no longer safe to be around. When He spoke to me, I ignored Him. I stopped telling Him my thoughts and I no longer watched Oral Roberts, fully convinced if I knew too much, God would cut short my life. Satan had deceived Adam and Eve to pull them away from fellowship with God and now he was insidiously and cunningly stealing me away from resting in my heavenly Father's arms.

Another diabolical blow came shortly after hearing the voice. Stumbling into the alcohol stash my parents had hidden below our kitchen sink, I discovered that when I drank Vodka, bad feelings temporarily went away. Through experimentation, I soon learned how much I could drink without my Mom or Dad's detection.

By the time high school rolled around, that first curious swig as a child had evolved into regular weekend partying. While other seniors in our rural community of several thousand were lauded at graduation for their personal accomplishments, I was notoriously becoming known as Rio Vista's 'town drunk'.

Natural Addiction, Supernatural Healing

Six weeks after dying and meeting the figure in heaven's tunnel entrance, I sat in the Striper Hotel lobby, inebriated and experiencing my fourth and final heart attack. At the hospital later that day, the doctor pulled me into his office and tearfully announced, "Rick, go home, get your affairs in order: you've got about six months to live. One of your heart's ventricles is pumping both ways - backward and forward - so it's not supplying blood to your body like it should." Then he added, "But, if you begin dieting and follow our regimen of care, you may live for as long as a year."

I answered him honestly, "Doc, I've tried to stop drinking for 10 years, but I can't. Just check me out and let me go home." More times than anyone could count, I had tried to quit drinking alcohol, but I could never make it through the detoxification period into sobriety. In my mind, I didn't *want* to be an alcoholic: I *had* to drink to survive.

One month later I returned for a follow-up appointment. Weighing in at 256 pounds, I was half drunk, with a distended stomach from alcohol and white as a sheet. As the doctor stared at an ex-ray of my heart, he remarked to me incredulously "Look at this! Your enlarged heart has shrunk one and a half inches in diameter! I'm sending you for more tests to see what's going on in there."

Several hours later I listened to the stunned cardiologist's findings. "Rick, I don't understand what happened, but your heart has shrunk and you now have the healthy heart of a 19 year old!" When I returned to present my doctor with the cardiologist's findings, I watched as he wrote across my medical chart "It's a miracle!". He turned and looked at me, shaking his head and mumbling, "This beats anything I've seen in my life!"

I'd been healed! Once again, God divinely intervened in the midst of my drunken living. This time, He completely restored my physical heart, a supernatural cure that would have thrilled any normal person. But as I left the doctor's office that day I felt only absolute despair. This gift from above felt like I'd just been cursed to live out a miserable lifetime sentence inside the prison walls of my own addiction. In heaven I'd felt glory, freedom and incredible peace, but if I couldn't stop drinking, what did I have to look forward to on this earth?

That afternoon I decided to bury the torment of my emotional pain by the only method I knew: getting thoroughly loaded. I carefully hid several bottles of alcohol in my clothing so the local police, who knew my drinking history, wouldn't confiscate them. Carrying my cache, I climbed the stairs to my hotel room. Each step seemed to loom up toward me as a wash of deep agony and desire weighed down my whole being. Somewhere between the lobby and my room on the second floor I crumpled onto my knees under the force of it all and cried out to my childhood Friend, "God! I can't do this anymore! Help me!"

Sober And Saved

That was my last day of inebriation. The following morning I called my parents and with the help of their friends, spent almost a month detoxing and receiving intense counseling at Peralta Hospital. Twenty-eight days later I was no longer saturated with alcohol, but actually sober for the first time in a very long time! I had made it through the challenges of drying out and was ready for reentry into the real world.

When the time approached to check out of the hospital and settle back into society, I had no intention whatsoever of ever returning to my hometown of Rio Vista, where I'd lost my wife and children because of drinking and in the process made a complete fool of myself as a functionally illiterate drunk. But near the end of my stay at Peralta, God spoke. Not audibly, but for the first time since my childhood I heard Him call to my spirit. "My son," He addressed me kindly, "If you can't make it in Rio Vista, what makes you think you can make it anywhere?"

Thinking of all the things I'd done and everyone I'd hurt, I knew in my own strength I could not go back to face people in my hometown. But God had come into my life once again, and He was directing me homeward. That was enough. Returning to Rio Vista, I began attending a little Pentecostal church I'd occasionally visited as an alcoholic. During those days I used to slip quietly into the back pew during praise and worship, then wave goodbye to the pastor and steal away during closing prayers before anyone had a chance to take note of the town drunk sitting in the service.

Now as a sober man, I willingly walked to the front of the same church during a Sunday service altar call, and recommitted my life to Jesus. Later in the meeting, pastor Darryl announced "We're gonna' do some baptisms in the Holy Ghost," and he looked straight at me. "Alright," I agreed, "but I'm not falling on the ground!" I wanted no part of that weird, demonstrative stuff. He prayed for me and suddenly I found myself looking up from the floor with Darryl leaning over me and whispering into my ear, "Rick, you don't have time. This is your prayer language. Use it until you get your own. You're baptized, now use your prayer language." He had me repeat phrases in tongues to use temporarily, until I received my own as a heavenly gift.

From that point forward my relationship with God took on an entirely new dynamic! The living presence of God was *in* me through His Spirit, and I found myself constantly interacting with Jesus. I hadn't experienced this kind of vital relationship with God since my childhood days.

Little by little I was becoming grateful to be alive, a complete turn around from all the previous years of desperation. In the Alcoholics Anonymous manual called "The Big Book," I had read a significant quote that, **"*our dilemma is lack of power*"**. As a believer, I was discovering *He* was my power, just as the Scripture said: *"...you will receive power when the Holy Spirit comes on you"*.[3] During all those years of inebriation I had lacked the strength to get sober and stay sober. Now I was experiencing His REAL power by achieving the unimaginable: sobriety after more than twenty years of alcoholism.

Sonship

Why were the dreams of a little eight-year old boy stolen through diabolical deception? How was I pulled into a lie that opened the door to the darkness of alcohol? Honestly, I don't know or fully understand the reasons behind the travesty of those years. What I DO know, is when I met the Holy Spirit, He began to teach me about God as my *Father* and to lead me in a

---

[3] *Acts 1:8, NIV*

process of restoring dreams that had been lost for so long. God was no longer a 'crisis' God who only intervened when I cried out in desperate circumstances. Now, His interactions with me held purpose: He wanted us to walk together as *Father and son.* He had dreams for us. My heart was awakening to the reality that God had committed to being with me forever!

His absolute devotion to me dawned gradually, through healthy human relationships. As a returning prodigal I was learning that human beings are meant to be in *community.* While drinking, I distained Alcoholics Anonymous meetings and judged those who attended them as a 'bunch of weak-minded drunks'. But God dealt with my pride and after sobriety, AA meetings and fellowshipping in church became the two main places of nurture in my life.

My *AA* sponsor, Richard Pelletier, was a strong believer whose mentoring challenged my old mind-sets of condemnation, self-hatred and fear. From the beginning, he had me write on a 3 X 5 card God's opinion of me, and instructed me to keep the card with me at all times. I wrote,

- *I am a rich child of a loving Father and I dare to prosper.*
- *I can to all things through Christ who strengthens me.*
- *No weapon formed against me can harm me.*[4]

These phrases became my mainstay and in those early days when I became angry or afraid, I'd take out my card and read these words until peace came. I was being trained to walk in the *truth,* replacing lies I'd believed for so many years. Even to

---

[4] *1 John 3:1; Jeremiah 29:11; Philippians 4:13; Isaiah 54:17*

this day, these three phrases are written on my heart in permanent spiritual ink, forever a part of the foundations of my salvation experience and my life.

Blessings of Discipline and Thankfulness

I remember thinking as a child that someday I would become the 'big boss' of my father's oil-drilling company. After becoming sober Dad gave me a job, but it was about as far away from being boss as you could possibly get. I was hired to sweep floors and clean cellar boards that had been pulled from old oil drilling holes. Cellar boards are where every swashbuckling, rough-and-tough field employee throws his garbage, where he spits, and even where he relieves himself. When the oil well runs dry, these boards are then pulled up and cleaned to use again in another frame for a different drilling hole.

Day by day in my new job, I pulled spikes from these filthy boards and scraped off all the mud and gunk. During the first week at the shop I angrily threw boards across the room, completely demoralized by my new assignment. I was doing my best, but the job wasn't doing anything to check my pent-up frustrations! Then one day a friend said to me, "If you learn to love those cellar boards, God will change things for you." I figured he was probably right, so instead of cursing the boards when I threw them across the room I began to say, "I love you, stupid board!" I imagine God was patiently smiling at my small effort towards an attitude change! But several days later when a misty rain was falling and the whole outdoor crew was laid off without pay until the rain stopped, I found myself actually *thanking God* for the opportunity to work.

During ten years of drunkenness I'd lost everything: my family, my driver's license, my vehicle, a place to live and my job. I'd even lost my health through being grossly overweight. Basics like taking care of personal property, learning to work regular hours at an occupation and losing weight through exercise became a new training ground in my Father's love. I was learning the essential lesson that sonship included healthy, personal disciplines. It wasn't easy and there were many days of battling anger at myself and at God for all I had lost, but He remained entirely patient. He knew what I needed in order to develop and faithfully brought me along at the right pace. God is never in a hurry.

Promotion

Finally calm in my soul, instead of throwing the boards at work, I started stacking them and saving the spikes for scrap metal. After a few weeks Dad and several of his foremen drove up to my work area in a brand new, outfitted yellow pickup truck. One of the men got out and announced to me, "Rick, we want you back out on the field. We need your help and expertise and we want to make you a foreman. Here's your work truck, and we're giving you a raise." With wisdom, my earthly dad added, "We're not giving you any *authority* right now: we're only giving you *responsibility*. Learn how to *lead* the men under you. Don't *push* them. If you learn how lead them, you'll be alright."

God loves to promote his children when they are ready in spirit and soul. Of course, the timing is always His and not ours, and after I had demonstrated faithfulness and thankfulness in the most humble of jobs, He chose to give me a new position.

For several years I served my father as a foreman in his company until, with his blessing, the time came to venture out on my own as a drilling contractor. Problem was, I had no capital, no drilling rig, no work crew and no financial backer.

As I talked with God about my desires, doors began to open. I met a man who agreed to recondition a used drilling rig. He even offered to wait to bill me for the cost of his work until after I had established a financial backer. While he began restoring the used rig, I contacted every possible investor in the area. Anxiety began to mount after several weeks passed without finding any interested parties. I'd stepped out in faith at a time when the industry's pace was slowing down and other drilling companies were going bankrupt. The crew that was rebuilding my drilling rig would soon need to be paid: I'd gone into debt and now I was scared!

Driving down River Road near home, I remarked to God, "Father, I think I missed you. People are afraid to risk backing me and the time doesn't seem right to start a business." As I rode along, I quietly came to the conclusion that the only option left was to sell everything and give up. "God, please help me sell all this equipment I've bought," I prayed.

Lord What do you Want me to do Now?

The Real Voice of God

For the second time in my life I heard an audible voice address me. The voice said aloud, "*My son, when you know these things come from Me, all things will be added to you.*"[5] The voice was so real, I automatically glanced at the passenger's seat to see if God was sitting there!

This time, unlike the enemy's audible voice of my childhood, I *knew* this audible voice belonged to Father God. His affirmation melted all my fears of mounting debt and I went home and slept peacefully that night. In the morning I asked Him, "Lord, what do you want me to do now?" He spoke to my heart, "Go and see George Cane."

> "My son, when you know these things come from Me, *all* things will be added to you.'"[1]

Now when God makes a discernable statement out loud, you'd think obeying Him would be easy. But George Cane was intimidating as a sharp, local businessman and CEO of his own company. Obediently but anxiously heading toward his office, I drove by the building three times before settling on a plan to write a note on the back of my business card and leave it with his secretary. That way if he didn't return my call, I was off the hook and no harm would be done.

---

[5] *Luke 12:31*

Pulling into the parking lot, I got out of my truck and walked towards the entrance, just as George himself opened the door and headed my way. "Hello Rick!" He quipped, "I want to talk to you! Come into my office!" When we sat down together he commented, "I don't know if you remember, but about three years ago you came here looking for a job and you were so drunk that when you opened the door of your truck, you almost fell out. Something has changed! What happened?"

I shared with George that I'd met Jesus Christ and had stayed sober because of His presence in my life. He continued by asking about my family, and after more small talk I couldn't stand it any longer and blurted out, "I need some help financially, George!" He responded, "How much? Five hundred thousand? A million?" I told him the amount and he looked at me and instructed, "Go to the bank and get the loan papers drawn up. I'll sign them for you."

Astonished at his generosity, I thanked him and walked toward the door to leave. Thoughtfully, George called after me, "Hey, have you got a work yard for storing all your equipment?" "No sir, not yet" I responded. "Well, don't get one. I've got 10 acres and I'll set you up there. Oh, and by the way, do you need an office?" His liberality was expanding. "Yes sir, I do," I answered truthfully. "Well, I'll have an office trailer brought over to the property, and we'll run electricity and phone for you as well. And do you have a secretary?" he asked. Again, I told him I didn't have one yet, and he said, "I'll send one of my employees to work for you. They can do your office work and answer phones for you until you get established. You just go and get that money and get moving." When I asked why he was being so kind, he motioned to all the things around him and replied, "What good is all this if I can't help someone now and again?"

My meeting with George was the first of many training experiences in understanding how God works to help us to fulfill our dreams. *Divine* and *natural elements* usually combine for a *supernatural result*. There is no "sonship formula" where we pray and suddenly, "poof!" things magically appear so we can immediately do great things in bringing the Kingdom of God to earth. There *are* miracles that occur, but usually the process is more akin to God giving guidance and pointing to provision, and our responding through stepping out in co-operation and risk.

> *Divine and natural elements usually combine for a supernatural result*

I watched almost surreally as *McKinney Drilling* became a reality and our company began to prosper. The audible promise of my heavenly Father was coming true: all things *were* being added to me. As we walked through nine years of business together, God was no longer a distant, ethereal concept somewhere up in the sky, but the One who delights and even *expects* to collaborate closely with humans.

Specific Answers From A Specific God

But as I said, God's provision through George Cane was only the first of many heavenly tutorials about God's ways. In another *naturally supernatural* circumstance, I learned that God knows us and loves to answer our prayers, even down to the finest details of our requests. Early on in my sobriety, I really wanted a boat and one day I asked my AA sponsor, "Hey, what if I want something for myself? I'm praying for all these other people, but what if I want to pray for something for me?" He encouraged me go ahead and present my requests to God, then added that I should pray *specifically* because **"specific prayers bring specific answers"**. That was all I needed to hear! Boldly, I laid everything out to God: "Lord, I'd like a flat-bottom, jet boat that's fast and has a big engine, thick carpets, all-leather interior, stereo throughout, and a nice trailer with "mag" wheels that exactly match the mag wheels on my new truck." I finished my request by asking God for someone who would be willing to finance the boat, since my credit had been destroyed through years of alcoholism.

One of my mentors had told me to make my request and then let it go and trust that God is a *good God* who will give me the desires of my heart in His way, and in His time. Excitedly, I gave everything to him and moved onto other aspects of my life.

Several months later a friend knocked on my door. He owned a boat shop and knew I'd been looking for a boat. "I think I've found something for you and it's pretty reasonable" he said. We drove to a local resort and walked out onto the dock. There in the slip lay an old day cruiser with a shoddy interior that needed an incredible amount of work. The engine was small and it didn't have a flat bottom and the trailer looked as bad as the boat. My heart sank as we stood there, but I thought to myself, *maybe this is where God wants me to start.* As I considered this option another thought entered my mind.

The Holy Spirit whispered to me, *that's not what you asked Me for; that's not what you prayed for.* I turned to my friend and said "Gene, I appreciate that you brought me down here, but this isn't what I prayed for." I had no idea whether Gene was a believer, but he looked at me and said, "I sort of thought you'd say that. I do have one more boat to show you."

Back at the shop he rolled back sliding doors to reveal a gorgeous, twenty-one feet day cruiser with a flat bottom, leather interior and thick carpets, stereo throughout, a Jacuzzi jet pump, large engine, nice trailer, and mag wheels that exactly matched the wheels on my pick up. Worth about $40,000.00, it perfectly lined up with all the specifics of my prayer request. But as I admired the boat, my automatic internal response doubted, *This is MUCH more than I can afford!* As if addressing my silent hesitation, Gene spoke up, "The man who owns this boat has to let go of it, but he still owes me about $7,500.00 in payments. Rick, if you can pay it off, you can have it."

His offer was incredible! Unfortunately, I still didn't have financing, so God would have to complete part two of my original petition: He would need to provide someone willing to risk giving me a loan. A few days later I sat in the office of a complete stranger whom Gene had suggested as a possible financier. I decided to be brutally honest. "I'll save you the effort of checking my credit report: I was a drunk for years and I don't have a lick of credit, but I have a good job now and I'd really like to buy this boat." After a little more discussion he sat up and looked at me, then at the paperwork and back at me. "I don't know why I'm doing this, but I'm going to give you the money for this boat. I believe you need to start over again and this will be a good way to establish your credit." He pulled out his checkbook and wrote me a check for $7,500.00.

Whatever!

Like Gene's first offer of the old rust-bucket boat, I learned very early in my new walk with God that before we receive *true* answers to our prayers for provision, we may receive a *counterfeit* of our original request. The battered-up boat fit

> **The Bible became the book of "I can"**

my old self-image perfectly and since the truth of my value to God hadn't yet completely permeated my new-believer heart, it would have been easy to compromise and make a concession by buying the old vessel. But when the Holy Spirit spoke, strength came to stand my ground and when I did, the *real* answer swiftly followed the counterfeit offer.

When I was living from a carnal mindset I saw the Bible as the book of "*I can't*": I can't do what I want; I can't go where I want; I can't receive these blessings; I can't successfully follow all these rules"! With this negative frame of reference I could only see liabilities to following God. But as a new Christian walking in agreement with His statutes and precepts, the Bible became the book of "*I can*": "*I can* do all things through Christ who strengthens me; *I can* ask and I will receive; *I can* pray specifically; *I can* succeed". A whole new world of possibilities came into being when I saw God's answers in my life, and the liabilities began to fade away. Many times I found I only had to *try* and it was enough to sense His favor, because whether I succeeded or failed, God's goodness honored my heart's intentions to please Him.

Jesus told His disciples *whatever* they ask for, if they believe they have received, it would be given to them.[6] Did He really mean *whatever?* Why would God want to give us *whatever we ask?* The answer lies in the context of intimacy. The Father shines with glory when His children 'bear much fruit'![7] Images come to mind of the Trinity - our Heavenly Dad and Elder Brother, and Holy Spirit - beaming with great pleasure when we carry out the Royal Family Business in the Kingdom. Their joy abounds because as a child in the Family, we are walking in the destiny they have created for our lives and they *love* when their children are happy and fulfilled!

Through God's presence and devoted love, my life had completely changed and my growing experiences of sonship were only the beginning. God was building in me a desire to give to others what he was so generously sowing into my life. Even before sobriety and throughout the early years of walking with God, I carried a seed of hope that someday I would run a recovery ranch for addicts and alcoholics. But before the ranch could become a reality, God had a surprise waiting. I would share the call with my future wife, Teresa, whose own freedom from addictions would qualify her to bring healing and help to the broken lives God would eventually send our way.

---

[6] *Mark 11:22-24*
[7] *John 15:8*

Knowing God:

Do you have a relationship with God? Have you received His Spirit into your life? If not, you can right now. Just invite God to come and be with you, praying something like this: *Jesus, thank you for taking my place on the cross and dying for my sins.[8] I ask now for your free gift of forgiveness and I receive your cleansing for every sin I have committed.[9] Please send Your Spirit into my life and make me part of your heavenly Family. I don't want to live life on my own any longer, so overflow into all me: wash away the old and create in me a new spirit.[10] I invite you to guide me and help me from this time forward, and to teach me what it means to be in relationship with you and with others who love you. Thank you, God!*

If you prayed this prayer for the first time, you have just become a child of God! This is only the beginning of a new, eternal relationship with Him!

---

[8] *2 Corinthians 5:21*
[9] *Hebrews 10:14-22*
[10] *Ezekiel 11:19*

For Further Reflection

1. As you look back over your life, have you sensed God's presence even at times when you were unaware? Thank Him for His care and provision. *Psalm 32:8*

2. Who has God said that you are? Ask Him to show you personally and write down the truths He reveals. Carry them with you and declare them over your life. *1 John 3:1*

3. Is there an area in your life where you have not yet broken into victory? How could thankfulness help to bring release? *Micah 2:13; Philippians 4:6,7*

4. Are there people in your life who provide healthy community for you, as well as guidance and wise accountability? If not, seek God about how to change your life in order to receive the blessings of godly friendship and counsel. Ask Him to show you where you 'fit' and be patient as He answers your prayer. If you're already relating to others as your spiritual family, take time to thank them in some way during the next week. *Proverbs 15:22*

5. List specific desires of one your life dreams and share them with God. Allow His answers to unfold and trust Him for His timing. *Psalm 20*

Prayer:

Thanks, Father, for watching over my life. I want to grow in intimacy with you: will you show me how to build our relationship? If there is anything standing in the way of my trust, I invite you to show me what I need to do in order for us to walk together closely. I want a life of dreaming, God. Lead me and I'll follow You into my destiny as your child! Together we will change my circumstances to agree with heaven.

Johnny Soliece Finds Solace

I woke up in a car somewhere in a back alley, craving enough *meth* to get high so I could make it through another day. As the haze of sleep slowly wore off, I realized my *homies* would be hunting for me, since we were deeply partnered in all sorts of illegal activities and I was 'obligated' to them. They'd probably already released their 'dogs', their patrol, to find me but in my twisted world, all I could think about at the moment was where I could get enough money to buy another fix of stimulating, satisfying *methamphetamines*.

Stopping over to see a Christian who'd always been kind to me, I hit him up for twenty bucks. As he handed me the money he began pleading with me to consider getting help for my drug addiction. "*New Hope Recovery Ranch* is a great place, Johnny. God loves you and He showed me He's got a good plan for your life." My Christian friend was so sincere. Normally, I would have politely feigned interest in his little spiel until I could break in with an excuse to leave. But on this particular day, I was sick and tired of my life. Sleeping in the back seats of cars, always aching for more meth, risking time in jail if I were caught: I hated all of it, so when my donor finished his pitch, out of my lips tumbled a half-hearted commitment to go to New Hope.

Thrilled, my friend agreed to somehow get me there the next morning. Though I'd been only partly sincere when I promised go into the recovery program, throughout the day I found myself saying goodbye to my kids, to my mother, and even to my homies. Sure enough, the next day I was on my way from California to Nevada, to be dropped off in the middle of what seemed like a God-forsaken land.

God was, in fact, very near to this land. With the help of the pastors, the ranch foreman and others, He began to break my old habits much like a cowboy goes about taming a wild stallion. For a while I kicked and bucked against all the rules and requirements: my time at the ranch wasn't easy and the transition away from a life that centered around drugs was slow.

But this wonderfully scrubby, dusty desert is where God and I met and where I learned to talk with Him. At the back of the men's house at New Hope, there is a spot that faces the hills and every morning at sunrise I would meet God there to praise Him or to cry and pour out hidden things in my heart. One day at that special place, I heard God say to me as clearly as any beautiful sound I've ever heard, *"John, I love you"*. Turning to face the hills, I was overwhelmed with gratefulness and cried in response, "Thank You, God, thank You for loving me!"

When the time came to leave the ranch I felt apprehension about a new, unfamiliar life. I couldn't go back to my old haunts and old friends because I wasn't the same person anymore. I'd lost everything by cutting off that life and as I crossed the desert to return to California, the only certainty I still held onto was that God would go with me.

When I left the ranch in 2006, I had nothing except my friendship with God. Since that time I have been restored to my wonderful wife and my two sons and we now have a lovely baby daughter. Jesus has given back what the enemy stole from my life, and has heaped on additional blessings of His favor. We are currently actively involved with our church fellowship in Costa Mesa and have the privilege of serving in several ministries, like helping provide meals for undocumented workers.

Jesus deserves all the glory for all we are and all we have been given. This coming June marks six years of recovery for me. I thank God for Rick and Teresa McKinney, who taught me to count the cost in all I do and to understand trials and struggles as a part of life that we walk *through* by God's grace, to come out into even greater purposes. Most of all, the McKinneys introduced me to my loving God, my Helper and the Maker of all things:

I lift up my eyes to the hills—where does my help come from? My help comes from the LORD, the Maker of heaven and earth.   Psalm 121:1, 2

2

FINDING TRUE LOVE

Teresa's Story

Out Of The Ashes

Somewhere during my forties I discovered the man I had called *father* for my entire life was not my biological father, a revelation that shed light on confusing heart messages I had tucked away in the recesses of my soul, like dusty old books that are quietly forgotten in ancient libraries. While growing up, I'd always felt dad doled out preferential treatment to my siblings but withheld affection from me and now I knew why: they were his birth children and I was not.

As a teen, I ran crying to him after being sexually molested by a man in our extended family. Having experienced a traumatic violation of my personal being, I just knew Daddy would rise up to defend me. Instead, I was crushed when he insisted that we tell no one to avoid stirring up trouble among our relatives. Choosing to protect the perpetrator rather than me cemented my belief that in Daddy's heart, I was less valuable, less important and less loved than others.

Feeling utterly abused and rejected, I struck out on my own in search of someone who would love me. Unfortunately, I had no idea what love should look like. Neither of my parents had grown up knowing wholesome examples of relational love and as a result, affairs and infidelity were a regular part of our family life. Since my definitions of dating were formed by their role modeling, I imitated the only pattern I'd known by assuming 'love' could be found through sexual promiscuity.

At the age of seventeen, I was pregnant. A young man had given affection to me through sexual intimacy and I welcomed the baby as part of a plan to start a new life with him, away from the struggles of our turbulent family life. Convinced I'd found love and happiness, Bob[11] and I eloped and settled into our own tiny apartment.

Religiously Speaking

Together, my new husband and I began attending a conservative church sect where fellowship and sincere friendships filled my heart with a sense of 'belonging'. For a while I was genuinely happy, thrilled to be a new mom, a wife and a 'sister' in a new spiritual family.

---

[11] *Not his real name*

Bob was quickly promoted to the illustrious position of *pastor* in our tiny congregation, but because the 'church' was too small to pay us a salary he continued to work part-time and to carry out ministry on evenings and weekends. Before long, he was spending less time at home and more time fulfilling various church activities, and the joy we'd had at the outset of our marriage ebbed away.

I was also becoming increasingly uncomfortable with occasional smiles or touches between Bob and several women in our church. Their exchanges felt far too familiar for pastoral care. Unmistakable evidence mounted and soon I knew my husband-pastor was having an affair. When I approached the church elders with suspicions of my husband's adultery, they looked at me and responded with a shrug. "He's the preacher. There's nothing we can do about it unless we have real 'proof'. But, if you divorce him you'll lose your salvation, so you'll just have to endure."

This particular sect taught divorce as an unpardonable sin that sends you straight to hell, unless there is unmistakable proof of adultery. And since my husband was our pastor, these elders sincerely informed me that as a 'good Christian' and faithful wife, I would simply have to live with the situation.

Devastated and fearing eternal damnation, I stayed. On one side of my own large emotional chasm was an unfaithful, unrepentant husband-pastor and on the other side, the gaping pit of hell. My life laid languishing somewhere in between, and thus began a pattern of silently enduring deep suspicions of my husband's numerous affairs. My own family was caught in the web of the sect's pharisaical religion and they too, promised to disown me if I 'disobeyed' God by breaking my wedding vows to leave my unfaithful spouse and my church.

Hiding Pain

For twenty-five years I lived hopelessly trapped in fear, until one day the agony of my life finally overpowered hell's threat. I'm not sure what tipped the scale, but at some point I'd simply had enough. I didn't *want* to go to hell, but if that was the requirement for escaping the present excruciating misery, I was willing to pay the price. I couldn't take one more day of my present torment.

By the time I walked away from our pseudo-marriage and the only 'church' I'd known for so many years, I had entirely given up on God, figuring if He was sending me to hell for divorce there was no use trying to relate to Him anymore. This God, the *god of law* I'd experienced through the sect's teachings, was impossible to please and entirely unjust. I was no longer certain He even existed.

I left everything. Family, friends, religion, belongings. By the time my flight reached the west coast where I was resettling to start another life, I was thoroughly drunk. After all, if I was already doomed to Hades, what was the harm of partying? Carousing and wild weekend bashes in my new life helped to cloud the emotional pain that throbbed internally whenever I was sober. Drugs, drinking and promiscuity hid the personal monsters in my closets of sadness, hopelessness and failure.

Two years passed and my drinking only escalated. Fully aware I was on a downward slide, I tried to quit numerous times, but alcohol always won every round of my fight towards soberness. One evening I took a walk along the beach, carrying a wine bottle and lost in troubled thought. I hadn't talked to God for years, hadn't read my Bible, and hadn't gone to church. I blamed God for losing my children to the 'church', and for the all those years when the 'church' ignored my protests about my husband's adulterous affairs. As a matter of fact, I blamed God for *everything*. But standing there in the sand by the ocean, a hundred pound burden of helplessness pressed me to the ground. Groaning welled up from deep within my spirit and I roared into the wind, "God, HELP ME!"

God's answers come in many forms and in this particular situation, He sent a friend who had seen me wandering along the surf, to find out if I was all right. We walked and talked for several hours, strolling along the water's edge. Since my friend knew if I went home I would only get more wine and drink myself to sleep, he asked, "Have you ever tried AA meetings?"

As far as I was concerned only drunks attended Alcoholics Anonymous and in my arrogance I wasn't about to call myself a drunk, even though I was half loaded with booze. I informed him of my opinions about 'those people', but somehow he still convinced me to go with him to that evening's local AA meeting.

Later, I sat in a gathering where every participant openly and honestly confessed former battles with addiction. Tears streamed down my face and I raised my hand, managing to choke out "I think I might have a problem with alcohol." I'd been binge drinking and doing drugs for two years and taking pills for much longer than that. The room full of strangers heard my desperate plea and piped up encouragingly, "Honey, you just keep comin' back one day at a time, and you'll be alright".

God of Friendship, God of Love

These strangers became supportive friends, and were the strength I needed to begin 'drying out'. Soon I was physically feeling better than I had in years, as the effects of alcohol and pills began to ebb from my body. Little did I know, but God – the real God, to whom I'd called for help - was preparing to meet me personally and lead me in a process of healing for my whole being: spirit, soul and body.

A man named Rick moved into the area and joined our meetings. Sober for quite a while, he attended AA to maintain healthy disciplines of accountability. Rick talked about his relationship with Jesus as if the two of them were bosom buddies. "God provided a parking space for me tonight!" He announced one evening and I thought to myself, *do you really think you're important enough that God would **talk** to you? And even give you a parking space?* From my own religious understanding, that kind of thinking was sheer arrogance!

All my life I had dreamed of meeting someone who would treat me tenderly and give me unwavering affection. Naturally then, when this new guy kept weaving stories of the personal interactions he and Jesus always seemed to have, I was intrigued. Driving to the store one day, I breathed a thought upward, *God, remember that crazy man who said you gave him a parking space? Would you do that for me?* Feelings of being such an unworthy sinner overwhelmed me and I couldn't even make my request out loud, but sure enough, when I pulled into the normally overflowing store parking lot, in plain view was *my* parking space that I had requested!

Soon that 'crazy man', Rick McKinney, gave me a copy of "Good Morning, Holy Spirit," by Benny Hinn. I'd been taught in my former religious dogma, that the Spirit of God was not a living *being*, but only the Word of God and no more: He was represented as an 'it' and not as our *Loving-Comforter-Nurturer God* and our *Dynamis-Power God*[12], who is an equal part of the Trinity. I sat in my kitchen

> **My spirit soared in hopes that God actually loved me**

sipping my morning coffee and reading Benny's testimony of falling in love with The Holy Spirit. *How can this be true?* I questioned, but my spirit soared in hopes that God actually loved me and wanted to spend time with me.

That day, I could only read a few pages at a time before stopping to weep. Read and weep, read and weep. *How in the world did I miss The Holy Spirit in the Bible all these years?* I couldn't believe I'd been so duped! Time and again, I'd call Rick to ask him about another new spiritual revelation that had previously been hidden from my understanding. Grief

---

[12] *"Dynamis" is the Greek word in Acts 1:8, describing the power we receive when the Holy Spirit comes into our lives.*

that I'd lost so much of my life to religious deception welled up in me and mixed with intense desire to discover more.

Cleansing And Healing

I hadn't read the Scriptures for several years, but one sleepless night during this time of spiritual awakening, I decided to open my old Bible. Scrawled notes from my previous life of legalism were written all over its margins and wreaked of doctrinal law. I leafed through the pages to the Psalms, deciding they were a safe place to start. As I began to read a Psalm out loud, suddenly, something *moved* in the room. With my natural eyes I glanced up from my book to see two huge shadows coming out from behind the bedroom door and leaving through the window. Years later I understood that God, through His spoken Word on my lips, had sent some demonic entities packing!

Later, one early morning as I sat down to read my Bible, I glanced up from my kitchen chair and saw a note on the fridge. Rick had written, "Forgive your ex-husband" and had placed the note there as a reminder to release my former spouse for his sins against my life. Until that moment I hadn't been ready, but finally I bowed my head and chose to forgive every sin he'd committed, each pain he'd inflicted. I handed it all over to Jesus and felt a wash of tears cleanse my face and my soul from years of bitter unforgiveness.

God was healing me, wooing me out of religion and loving me back to life. Many days I sat on the beach near my house, talking to Him and reading my Bible. The Trinity and I were getting to know each other, even though there were times I felt overwhelmed that God would think about me, after all the sinful things I'd done. One day I spontaneously belted out a Celine Dion love song to Jesus and it dawned on me that I was no longer looking for the perfect guy whose affection would satisfy my strong craving to be loved. I had found *God* as the Lover I'd been seeking for my whole life!

Falling In Love, Part Two

Ironically, it wasn't long after this realization that I also began to fall head-over-heels for Rick, the man who had introduced me to the true and loving, real God. We had so much fun together, settling into the sand by the ocean, holding Bibles in one hand and coffee cups in the other. Local police officers, accustomed to seeing the two of us hunkered down along the surf on warm, quiet evenings, dubbed us the "Bible-reading crowd".

Though I'd been in a marriage for twenty-five years, never before had I encountered Spirit-filled interaction where my human spirit met another human's spirit in true and godly intimacy. Deep affection was an entirely fresh and delightful experience since, for the first time in either of our lives, we were basing a dating relationship on God's love and presence. The joy of the Lord was becoming our strength and the days of personal struggles were beginning to fade.

Regardless of how much we loved each other, we were still terrified of marriage. We'd both been in relationships where drugs, alcohol and affairs destroyed almost every aspect of our capacity to trust another person deeply. But after several years of growing spiritually and personally, Rick and I knew God was calling us into covenant relationship and we were married in a quiet, private ceremony. Our hope and faith were such that we sensed this time would be different: now we were *in God* and He would be the Covenant-Keeper to enable our faithfulness to each other.

> **God was healing me, wooing me out of religion and loving me back to life**

The day after our wedding ceremony, we drove to a little town called Silver Springs, Nevada, to dream. As we stood looking at a small plot of desert land filled with nothing but shrubs and an occasional jackrabbit, we envisioned a *recovery ranch* sitting on the property. Rick and I had both come through our own recovery from addiction and now God was stirring our hearts to help others find the same freedom for their lives. Imagining addicts and alcoholics living on the dry, dusty lot we were praying over, we saw ourselves helping them find sobriety and introducing them to their own vital relationships with the Holy Spirit!

We had discovered that God's love was the answer to embracing life. Two former alcoholics, filled with the New Wine of God's Spirit, in love with each other and in love with God, we had no means for making our dream come true. But we were just crazy enough to believe God would guide and provide, and with faith we jumped into the saddle together and rode into the desert to follow our Adventurer-God wherever He would lead. We were about to discover His pathway is filled with heaven's divine justice, redeeming our past personal losses by leading many others to victory and healing.

For Further Reflection

1. Has God answered your prayers through other people in your life? Thank God for them and consider sending them a note of thanks. *Psalm 91:15*

2. How does forgiving those who have hurt us bring healing to our own hearts? Consider Jesus' parable about forgiveness in *Matthew 18:21-35.* According to verses 34 & 35, how does unforgiveness cause personal torment? Ask God whether there is anyone you need to forgive. Be thorough and specific. Then release them to God and be sure to receive Father's comfort and healing love where you have experienced pain. For your own safety, even though you have forgiven, when another person has violated or broken your trust, healthy interactions may or may not be re-established. Forgiveness is a *heart* matter: human trust is *earned* by mutual honor and integrity.

3. Who is the Holy Spirit to you? How does the Holy Spirit comfort us and nurture us? How does He help us, for example, in our study of the Bible or in knowing truth? How is He love for you? Meditate on these verses and share your responses with Him: *Romans 15:30; 2 Corinthians 13:14; John 14:14-17, 26; John 7:38, 39; Ephesians 3:16 and Jude 1:20.*

4. How could bringing freedom to other addicts and alcoholics be a form of '*heavenly divine justice*' for Rick and Teresa's past personal losses? Ask God what heavenly justice for personal loss could look like in your life. Share His answer

with another believer. Pray together for God's justice to come to pass in your life.

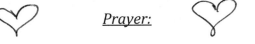

Prayer:

Holy Spirit, I want to be close to You and to know You intimately. Thank You for living in me: teach me how to hear Your voice and show me what it means to be Your friend, walking with You day by day. Bring me close to You and enable me to see life as an adventure with You inside me, for me, and through me!

Changing lives

Addicts aren't the only ones impacted by their habits: their loved ones are also incredibly affected, as you'll see by the testimony of Morre Hughes and her husband, Derek Hughes. Freeing an individual from addiction is the first step toward healing spouses, children and friends who have also been harmed by cycles of obsession and compulsion. Once an addict is restored, family foundations can be rebuilt and generational patterns renewed. To read Derek Hughes' testimony, turn to page seventy five..

Morre Hughes' Testimony

Sometimes good things come in small packages, but the first time we pulled onto New Hope's property I was convinced we'd made a mistake in reading our directions. Far from my city-slicker image of a luxurious spread with rolling green hills and lush pastureland, this understated, dusty ranch set in the middle of nowhere, was about to turn our lives around.

Months prior to coming to New Hope, my husband begged me to help him locate and check into an alcohol and drug rehabilitation center. We decided to try the Veteran's Administration. After all the necessary paperwork had been filled out, the VA accepted Derek and he settled into their facility for several weeks of detoxification.

I returned home to find a complete financial mess. My husband had always taken responsibility for our book-keeping and when I opened his records, the effects of his addiction on our resources leaped off the pages like a messenger of doom, announcing imminent economic ruin. Our bank account was eight hundred dollars overdrawn; all our bills were past due; our mortgage payment was six months in arrears, and the utility companies were planning to shut off our power and water because both accounts were delinquent. Added to all of this was the fact that I was five months pregnant with our first child.

We'd been married for ten years and during that time my husband had changed into a man I barely recognized, one entirely consumed by addiction. Preoccupied by his need for another 'fix', Derek threatened to leave me unless I helped him get drugs. In his desperation for another hit, he even said he didn't care if he ever saw me, or our unborn child, again. In an effort to keep my husband alive and present in our home, I agreed to do things I thought I would never do and went places I never should have visited. Like Derek, I had also become a different person in my futile attempts to save our marriage.

Desperation
When the VA facility put Derek on suicide watch I was scared, especially since he'd already failed at earlier attempts to detoxify. Picking up the phone, I called Rick McKinney at New Hope. I'd spoken with Rick a few times previously and he had agreed to take Derek into the ranch's program in spite of pending legal issues stemming from his addiction. But Derek had flat out rejected the idea of going to the ranch, announcing to me "I am not going there to work for free all day long."

I was desperate, sensing two choices remained: if the ranch didn't work, I felt my husband would die. The breaking point had arrived for Derek, for our marriage and for our family: God had spoken that much to me. Finally, my husband came to his wits' end and relented. The VA wasn't working for him and there were no other options.

Transitions

After my husband was at New Hope for a few weeks, I visited the ranch during a Sunday morning fellowship time. Derek' face was visibly different. He had accepted Christ as His Savior and his internal darkness had begun to fade, allowing God's light to shine through.

Such a glorious transition in him made me realize something was missing in my own life. I'd always believed in Jesus as my Savior, but now God invited me into a *relationship* with His Son.

My husband eventually graduated from New Hope's program. He's been sober for twenty months and we've become active in our new church home, Destiny Christian Center, in Reno. Now we help in reaching out to others who need the same kind of helping hand that was so lovingly extended to our family.

I am happy to say we are both living a life pleasing to the Lord and Calin, our beautiful baby boy, is being brought up in a solid Christian home. We couldn't be more grateful to Rick and Teresa McKinney for all that has transpired since we have been found by God's love. Most of all we give thanks to our heavenly Father, who has restored us, given us hope and a whole new spiritual family. We are a testimony of His glory.

3

GROWING PAINS

God Is Good, Even When Life Is Messy

Between the time of my detoxification and subsequent recommitment to Jesus in Peralta hospital, and the day I met Teresa ten years later, I experienced a failed marriage, bankruptcy in my business and numerous setbacks in my spiritual life. While going through the pain of divorce, I even started drinking again for a short period of time.

I would love to tell you that meeting God as my Father automatically made me like Jesus, a model son who listened perfectly to the Father and followed His every lead. The truth is, during the early days of being a Christian I probably stumbled and fell more than I actually walked! Like a toddler transitioning from crawling to standing up, I often found myself face down against the pavement with a bruised nose and a hurt heart. God would pick me up and wipe off the pebbles from my hands and I'd start to walk again, only to fall when I hit another bump in the road.

Several years after my salvation, pastor Darryl moved out of the area and our church fellowship dwindled to only a few people. Another primary spiritual father, my AA mentor, died and went to be with Jesus. In part because of these losses, my personal accountability became intermittent. Though I desperately needed Christian love in order to continue healing places of my heart that were still un-renewed by God's Spirit, interactions with other believers faded. My time with the Holy Spirit and time in His Word also decreased.

Often our wounding by authority figures (father, mother, teacher, church leader) will cause us to question whether God's authority is entirely good. As a result, we hesitate to *listen carefully* to what He has to say. One of the translations of the word *obedience* in the Bible is none other than that: *to listen carefully.* When we know God is perfectly good, we'll listen carefully and obey His advice with our whole heart. But not understanding that God *always, always, always* wants what's best for us, we often doubt His motives and ignore His voice.

Unfortunately, my trust in God's goodness was still being established and there were times when I doubted His intentions toward me. As a result, I tended not to listen to Him and since my connections with other believers and connections with the Spirit of God were no longer a regular part of the checks and balances I needed, my spiritual vision became skewed and choices I made weren't always from a place of seeing and hearing God.

Since those early years I've become convinced of God's goodness, but even when I wasn't sure of His kind intentions toward me, God was utterly faithful. He never withdrew His fathering or His love, and eventually His plans for our lives came to pass, in spite of our weaknesses and failings.[13]

Bankruptcy

After becoming established in my oil drilling business, I began to prosper. In addition to buying a cool recreational boat I eventually owned my own home, learned to fly airplanes, golfed regularly and even became the owner of a second successful business. Profits were multiplying and I was on my way to becoming financially secure.

But my *spiritual* bank account, where *things of the heart* are stored up as heavenly treasure, was looking rather lean.[14] Like a rusty old sparkplug, the contact between God and me had gotten 'gunked up' and I was losing sight of the fact that it was God who had prospered my businesses. Driving home from a business meeting in which I had just secured a large financial deal, a thought crossed my mind, *Look what you've done!* Just as quickly, the Holy Spirit's conviction gripped my heart and I confessed tearfully, "Oh, Lord, I didn't mean it!" But in truth, I had become proud.

---

[13] *Romans 8:28*
[14] *Matthew 6:19-21*

Listening to gods Voice

There is a king in the Bible named Nebuchadnezzar, who became extremely proud of his vast kingdom and took to himself all the glory for his accomplishments.[15] I became like Nebuchadnezzar and forgot that my blessings were a gift from God.

In less than eight months I sat in bankruptcy court, through betrayal by a business partner. God had allowed me to lose everything He'd given me. As the Scriptures teach, my pride had preceded a big fall.[16] Now, I don't believe for a second

> **God was utterly faithful**

that God caused my businesses to fail or that He designed the betrayal of a business partner to bring my harm. But pulling away from Him over time caused insensitivity to His voice and made me vulnerable to spiritual attack that often comes through the mind. Had I stayed close to the Lord, He could have dealt with the pride in my heart, through our regular interactions as Father and son. Instead, when I strayed away I no longer heard His course corrections for my life and the enemy was able to influence my thoughts.[17]

Hebrews 4:12 says that God's word knows the intentions of our minds and hearts. His word isn't just ink on paper: *He* is the Word, the spiritual power that discerns what comes out of our heart and mind, and what comes from our spirit. That's why staying close to the Lord and listening to what He says -

---

[15] *Daniel 4:19-37*

[16] *Proverbs 16:18*

[17] *2 Corinthians 10:4,5*

both the written word and the words the Holy Spirit speaks to our spirits - is essential in order to keep us on course and to keep our hearts protected from the 'god of this age', who is described as a destructive 'roaring lion'.[18]

Direction Toward Greater Purpose...Eventually

Throughout my years of thriving businesses, God had begun to put into my heart the idea of establishing an addictions recovery center for men who were trapped by alcohol. He'd given me much through my own spiritual mentors and I wanted to give back to others what I had so generously received. Several times I even went so far as to check out possible building sites that were for sale, but my businesses and profits took priority and my dream sat dormant in the back of my mind.

When my companies came crashing down like a house of cards, the idea of a recovery center was still very far from my mind: I just wanted a job. Yet in God's economy, a career switch was the very thing that would bring Teresa and me together and awaken desires in the direction of a recovery center. Losing everything was the gateway to a whole new focus filled with purpose and hope.

That's just like our good Father. Even when we don't have a clue where we're headed or how to get there, God is *entirely able* to direct the pathways of His children toward ultimate

---

[18] *2 Corinthians 4:4; 1 Peter 5:8*
[19] *Psalm 138:8; 2 Thessalonians 2:16,17*

fulfillment.[19] I found employment as a sales manager for a roof maintenance company that gave an option of changing locations, and I decided to head west. Years before, I had casually remarked to God "Someday I'd love to have an office in San Francisco, within walking distance of Fisherman's Wharf". Daily lunches on that wharf seemed like fun.

Like a dream come true, within a year I secured a suitable office situation near the Wharf. Everything was exactly as I'd once expressed in prayer to God, except for one startling difference. My new office happened to be smack in the middle of the 'Tenderloin', the most decadent area of San Francisco. Here in a center of business and finance, the streets were filled with drug dealers, prostitutes, peep shows, perversion and, not surprisingly, alcoholics and addicts.

> **God is entirely able to direct the pathways of His children.**

Suddenly, on a daily basis I was faced with the needs of those broken by alcohol, and every vision I'd had in the past of making a difference now found a place to be activated. Walking to my office each morning, I began to build friendships with the homeless men who lived on these streets. Most were addicted to something and as we became acquainted on a first name basis, I invited them to stop in at my office if they wanted prayer or needed help. Quite a few men came knocking on my door and during the time I worked in this district many were reunited with their families after years of estrangement.

Tiger Jones

One day as I passed by their sidewalk hovels I announced, "Hey, I'll pay whoever wants to help me move some furniture". I knew money for food came hard for them but even so, no one responded immediately. After a few seconds little Tiger Jones, with a voice that sounded like he'd swallowed the gravel he had slept on, slowly rattled, "I'll help you."

Tiger settled into the front seat of the pickup truck between Teresa and me, reeking of alcohol and months of accumulated body odor. Now eighty-three years old, he'd once seen his own wife and children cruelly murdered and the trauma had sent him beyond the edge of normalcy, into a long life of alcoholic wandering. He drank heavily and was addicted to heroin, but I liked this short, wiry man.

I hadn't said anything to Teresa, but I really wanted to help Tiger get sober and as the three of us rode side by side in our pick up truck, I silently hoped, in spite of his incredibly strong smell and the scabies on his skin, she would be willing to reach out to this likeable older gentleman. Later when we were alone, as if she'd read my thoughts, Teresa turned to me with concern "Rick, we need to do something for this man. He really touched my heart." Quietly hoping for a positive response I asked, "Do you think we need to let him live with us?" Teresa's tears flowed with compassion. "Yes, he stinks. Clean him up a little bit and get him some new clothes, and it'll be alright." She was filled with mercy, but we also knew the process of transitioning from drunk to sober wasn't easy and the next few weeks would present challenges for all of us.

Tiger Jones became the first of many to come into our home addicted and to leave 'clean'. Priority number one was to scrub him up and wash away layers of odor and grime so we could stand to live together in the same apartment! Next, we bought him a cowboy hat, boots, jeans and a collection of other clothing items and finally, over the following week, we helped Tiger detoxify. By God's grace he had no seizures or other physical reactions and soon his body and mind were beginning to clear from the poison he'd been voluntarily drinking and shooting into his system for such a long time.

Healing The Heart

My friendship with God had grown incredibly during recent years and now, both Teresa and I wanted to share with Tiger the same divine Lover who had found us in the midst of our need. No longer homeless, this little old man had seen love in action through our willingness to invite him into our lives. Now, Tiger needed to meet the source of all true love.

Unfortunately, through the trauma of his life he had sealed up his heart and was unwilling to let anyone find the real man hidden deep inside. Like so many addicted men and women, Tiger guarded his heart well and closed himself within thick walls of emotional protection.

Tiger needed animal interaction. Will Rogers once said "There's nothing like the outside of a horse for the inside of a man" and personally, I could vouch for his statement. My own AA sponsor had taught me how to work with horses on his ranch: to saddle them, clean their hooves, brush them and get them ready to ride. In my early sobriety I was angry about everything, but by the time I'd finished working with a horse, pent up anger toward myself, life and even toward God had dissolved and I could see blue sky and feel a renewed calmness in my soul. Animals have a way of touching and opening the inside part of an addict's heart that humans may struggle for years to reach.

We took Tiger to spend time with Maggie, our ornery old horse who was hard to ride and could be as cantankerous and stubborn as a donkey. One day we were leaning up against an old hay trailer, watching her graze. As I related to Tiger how bad-tempered Maggie could be, I noticed tears were streaming down his face. He'd been watching her in the pasture and quietly observed, "I can tell you exactly what's the matter with that horse." I waited, not wanting to do or say anything to spoil the moment. He continued, "I think maybe her mom and dad treated her bad. Maybe she never got any positive strokes. Maybe she was owned by people who neglected her and even beat her."

> *God loves when our dreams are bigger than our own abilities to fulfill them*

Tiger had pegged Maggie correctly. She had been abused and neglected and no one had played with her or treated her kindly. Horses are meant to live in herds and Maggie had been kept alone in a pasture, mostly ignored as though she were no more than a decorative ornament for her owner's farm.

This abused, neglected man had opened his heart to an abused, neglected horse. From that time on, we went to the stalls often. Tough Tiger couldn't wait to play with Maggie, feed her, touch her, talk to her. Maggie responded to his attention and warmed to his touches, as Tiger *loved* that horse. Gradually, Tiger's softened heart also opened to us and we were able to share with the real man inside of him: the one who, like Maggie, needed to be loved and praised and encouraged. Eventually, he met Jesus personally and received the comforting, strengthening, infilling presence of the Holy Spirit into his life.

Draw The Ranch

Tiger lived with us for three months before moving on, but our experience with him awoke in us a burning passion to buy a property that could adequately house several men at a time. We wanted to multiply our efforts so that more men could begin new lives. Pastureland and animals became part of our wish list, since we'd seen firsthand that horses, dogs, cattle, all sorts of creatures could reach the deeply wounded with unbiased love. In short, we wanted a ranch!

Someone once said, *nothing happens in the kingdom of God without first releasing it through prophetic declaration and prayer.* One day Teresa said, "Rick, draw the ranch you see in your spirit". I sketched the whole vision onto a large piece of paper. I saw the placement of corrals, of our house and a second house nearby for those in recovery, of the stalls for horses and small barns for other animals like goats or sheep. The sketch in my hands was a prayer released into heaven, a

70

seed planted in the Spirit realm that set into motion provisions for an actual, physical ranch to come into being.

God loves when our dreams are bigger than our own abilities to fulfill them, since He wants to partner with us in bringing them to pass by His supernatural power. The trek of faith we were about to embark on in order for our dreams to take shape would be hair-raisingly exhilarating and never dull. God found great pleasure in providing miraculously as we began to run with the vision. He had guided us both through years of wandering and now Father God was ready to plant us firmly into the soil of our 'promised land'.[20]

For Further Reflection

1. When have you seen and experienced God's *goodness* in your life? Write down your answers and talk to God about how He's shown you kindness and favor as His child (Titus 3:4-7). If you have any doubts about His goodness, ask the Holy Spirit to help you recognize, experience and receive His goodness in the coming weeks and months. Find a concordance and look up Scriptures on God's goodness that you can contemplate and/or memorize.

2. What has God's *guidance* looked like in your life? Together with Father God, reflect on Psalm 23, a Psalm that promises guidance in every situation. Here are several other

---

[20] *Joshua 1:11*

scriptures about guidance that will also encourage you: John 16:13; Psalms 25:4-6; Psalm 31:3; Ps 73:23-28; Isaiah 49:8-10.

3. In chapter one's reflection questions, you presented one of your life dreams to God. As you are in prayer with the Holy Spirit, look into your heart and express a dream once again, this time *creatively*. Choose an aspect of the same dream as before, or express a new one through writing, sketching, painting, singing, even dancing as king David once danced (2 Samuel 6:14)! God is the Creator, after all, and your creativity rises to Him as a powerful, prophetic release.

4. Understanding that obedience often means *listening carefully*, think about one time when you were able to hear God and respond to His voice for your life. What was the benefit for you? Ask the Holy Spirit to give you several practical and concrete ideas to apply *listening to Him* more carefully. Make a plan to practice one or more of the concepts He gives you, each day for the next week. You'll be encouraged by the results!

5. We have all been hurt in some way and have needed healing. Are there any areas of wounding in your life that keep you from believing you are a royal, loved child of God? In prayer, ask God to show you what lies you may have believed about Him or about yourself. If He reveals a lie, first repent for agreeing with the enemy, who is called the 'father of lies'. Reject the lie (out loud) as well as the spirit behind the lie. Then ask the Holy Spirit, "Holy Spirit, please show me your truth in place of this lie". Listen quietly for His answers. He will speak truth to you directly, through

one of your five senses (you may see a picture in your mind, hear a thought in your mind, sense a feeling, or experience a physical sensation or aroma). The truth you hear must line up with Scripture: that's how you know it's from God. Share what He tells you with a trusted, mature believer who will rejoice with you!

If you have been greatly wounded or abused and realize you need help, contact your church or a Christian counseling center and allow God to heal you through other more mature believers. God is waiting to reveal to you His absolute love! One such source for healing is Bethelsozo.com

Prayer:

Father God, thank You for bringing me into Your family through Jesus. As Your child, I want to experience the fullness of Your incredible goodness. Where I haven't been able to trust, please lead me to healing.

Holy Spirit, enable me to listen carefully to You and to honor Your Word as a map for my life. You are completely powerful to lead me in the paths You've prepared for us to walk together. Give me a revelation of Your dreams for us! Guide me into Your best for me and for my family.

The Saving Of Derek Hughes

There was a time when the value of my life was directly proportionate to the size of the dope bag or pill bottle I held in my hand. As a hardcore junkie and alcoholic, life was all about survival from one fix to another. Powerless to fight my addictions, I lived in a world of deceit and dishonesty. I lied to myself about my reality, I lied to my wife, family and friends, all for the sake of satisfying my craving for drugs.

Eventually, life became a revolving door from rehabs to jails and finally, to hospitals. No matter what I did or where I went I could not stay sober, and toward the end of that existence I overdosed on drugs. Except for God's mercy, I would have died.

When I arrived at New Hope Recovery Ranch I was beaten down physically, mentally and spiritually. My wife and mother had driven me there, and as their car pulled away and left me standing among strangers, I had no idea how I would pull through or what life would look like when I was no longer doped up or inebriated. Having been a user for so long, being sober seemed unfamiliar and even frightening.

Jesus Christ was the answer. We often hear that, but easily forget how much it rings true. Personally, He was the power I needed for deliverance from the compulsive desires that always dragged me back into drugs and alcohol. Even so, getting sober was a very painful and difficult process. There were many tough days and long nights at the ranch, learning how to follow directions, obey rules and live life without drugs.

Recovery became a journey to discover who I was as a person and more importantly, who I was *becoming*. I didn't know myself because my identity had always been associated with my habit. Getting honest about the things in my life that contributed to addiction required facing feelings of shame, emotional lies and other hurts that weighed me down.

Working through *The Twelve Steps & Spiritual Disciplines* slowly lifted the hopelessness that contributed to my life as a user. The dividends were incredible, leading me away from slavery to addictions and toward *sonship*. Intimate and personal interaction with God laid the basis for my new identity.

At New Hope, we were given principles of the Word of God and the presence of His Spirit. Values were instilled which have become foundations for my new life. The truths I learned there have helped me achieve long term sobriety and have defined my present walk with God.

Life is a lot different than when I first showed up as a broken shell of a man on the doorstep of New Hope. I'm a proud father and loving husband and once again a respected member of my extended family. Presently, I'm also a full time student working on an engineering degree. Everything the devil stole through drugs and alcohol has been restored to me by God, and now I live a life full of hope and love. The Holy Spirit has given back my self-worth, and my word has once again become trustworthy. In my wildest dreams, I couldn't have imagined the blessings God has poured into my life. Our family is living proof that He is *good!*

4

RISKING WITH GOD

We stood among acres of nothing but wild Nevada desert sagebrush, imagining the placement of every building and corral of the ranch that I'd sketched prophetically several months before. Kneeling down on the dusty soil, we prayed, "Lord, we believe this is the land for the ranch so we ask you, please give us this place."

But because of my business collapses ten years earlier, I carried a bankruptcy on my credit report and as Teresa and I returned to the real estate office that had directed us to this property, we began to wrestle with doubts. Our present net financial worth was a mere two paychecks. We had great jobs, but no money for a down payment and no investors, and the only 'treasure' we held was a sense that God had placed this desire in our hearts.

Having been involved in the business world, we both knew how to properly establish a financially successful enterprise. If someone had approached us and said, *"Um, hello, we would like to buy a manufactured home and place it on a ten acre property, but we have no finances. Oh, and once we move here, we won't have jobs either, but we are trusting God to provide for us:"* as investors, we would have thought this kind of attitude was crazy! Yet, this is exactly how we were operating.

We could have established an addictions recovery center more easily by accepting federal, county and state funding. But even while the ranch was still a dream I'd sensed God leading me not to tie it into governmental regulations. Instead, we were to function autonomously in order to create a place where the baptism of the Holy Spirit was the power for each resident's freedom from addiction. I also sensed we were not to charge a fee to the men who were entering our program: in every way, we were to trust God to provide.

Walking On Water

Surprisingly, we were quickly approved for a mortgage to purchase both the land, *and* a manufactured home. But now what? Even with mortgage approval, how were we to live? We needed wise counsel. Contacting Kay Peterson, the pastor at

Silver Springs Christian Center, we asked if we could meet and discuss with her our concerns about the financial risks involved with the whole ranch endeavor. Kay was a personal friend and as she listened later that day, she looked straight at us and answered "Rick, Peter had to *get out of the boat* before he could walk on water."

In the Bible, Matthew wrote that Jesus walked on top of the water across an angry sea, to meet his disciples in their boat.[21] Peter, one of Jesus' bolder followers, heard the Lord invite him to walk on the waves. He jumped out and walked on the water toward the Master, figuring "If Jesus invited me, that's all I need" and by *risking* he performed the impossible, alongside of His God!

> **Peter had to get out of the boat before he could walk on water**

Kay's comment hit me squarely in my heart. She was encouraging us that it was finally the right time for Teresa and me to jump out of the comfort of our 'boat', leave our careers, walk away from our present means of provision and step onto the foamy sea of faith and adventure in following God.

Having no idea how the finances would work out, we made the decision to resign from our jobs and through a family member, borrowed the $13,000.00 necessary for a down payment. In short order, we became the new owners of a manufactured home set humbly in the middle of the Nevada wilderness, on ten acres of gray earth and stubby sagebrush.

---

[21] *Matthew 14:22-34*

One Step At A Time

New Hope Recovery Ranch, the name we'd created to embody our vision, now existed. As we began to share our personal testimonies and laid out our plans to help others find freedom from addictions, generous believers started contributing financially toward the work. Before long, we'd received enough provision for our first month's mortgage payment and even had some money to spare.

Praying on the property one day shortly after we'd moved there, I asked God, "What do you want us to do first to establish the ranch?" He answered, "Build the fences." We'd brought our two horses, Maggie and Pokey, away from their lush California pastureland and they needed to be able to run freely rather than being harnessed and tied.

Taking another step of obedience and risk, we figured out how many posts, how much wire, staples, railroad ties and additional supplies we'd need. Then, using every single dime that remained after making our first mortgage payment, we drove to the local supply store and placed an order.

A few days later the delivery truck dumped a whole pile of goods onto our front yard. I was thrilled that our ranch was about to take shape and form, but Teresa was anxious. She couldn't possibly imagine how we were going to dig all those fence post holes or string all that wire, especially since snow still covered the winter desert's floor and the temperatures were frigid enough to make working outside a challenge. The task seemed entirely daunting.

I walked outside after hearing her apprehensiveness. "Lord, Teresa needs a sign. Please show her you're with us and that you'll help us." Praying for a while longer, I finally walked back into the house to encourage her. As we were sharing together I casually glanced out the window and there in the middle of a bright, cloudless desert sky was a large rainbow stretching over the road near the entrance of our new property. Seeing no rain anywhere on the horizon, all of Teresa's fears melted away when she realized God had created His sign of *covenant faithfulness*, in an absolutely sunny sky.[22] God confirmed our steps prophetically and we knew that somehow, our fences would be built.

Soon the youth group of Silver Springs Christian Center arrived on our property with tools and lots of energy, ready to string wire. Pastor Kay had suggested making the whole day fun by throwing a barbeque into the mix. When everyone left that evening with full stomachs and sore muscles, we'd made progress but still had a long way to go. Since we'd rented a post-hole digger for seven days at a great price, time was of the essence: we needed more help if we were going to finish the fences before returning the digger.

Fulfillment Of A Dream

In the middle of our fencing dilemma, the phone rang. Dallas Ramsey, the director of Center Street Mission in Reno, asked if we could help a young man who needed to get clean from his

---

[22] *Genesis 9:13-16*

addictions. Hal[23] lived in a nearby city and had been raised by alcoholics in an abusive home. He'd become an alcoholic like his parents and now wanted out of his destructive lifestyle. Dallas was calling to ask if the ranch was ready to receive residents.

We agreed to invite the young man into our home and hopped into the car to go and pick him up from the mission. While there, Dallas gathered up a collection of canned goods, pastas, cereals and more from the mission's food pantry and tossed them into our vehicle. Driving home with Hal in the back seat and groceries filling the trunk, Teresa noticed a birthday cake with one candle had been placed next to her in the passenger's seat. Sensing there was some significance to the candle, she quietly asked, "Lord, what is this? Are you saying something?" Immediately the still, small voice of the Holy Spirit responded, "Today is the beginning of the ranch. *Happy birthday!* Hal is your first man."

> *The spiritual fulfillment of our own visions and promises had snuck up on us while we were following God with fervent hearts*

We arrived home and the phone rang a second time. Kay Peterson was on the other end of the line. "Hi Rick, I've got three hitchhikers who need a place to stay. They slept outside at the lake last night and came to the church hungry and looking for food and money. I told them about your ranch. They could

---

[23] *We've changed names of the men who joined our recovery ranch and whose stories are recounted here, for the sake of honor and privacy*

help you with your fences and I think you will probably be able to help them with their alcoholism." Several hours later we sat around our dining room table with four famished alcoholic/addicts, a stash of food and a birthday cake to celebrate the very first day of our recovery ranch!

The spiritual fulfillment of our own visions and promises had snuck up on us while we were following God with fervent hearts. Our long awaited recovery ranch had quietly arrived in the form of four needy men. After years of hoping and praying, our dream was actually coming to pass without fanfare, formality or even much experience on our parts. Hal and the three hitchhikers, Devin, Tim and Willy, needed our help and we simply had it in our hearts to answer their needs and bring them to their Divine Helper.

Dreams, prophetic words and answered prayers are an interesting phenomena. While we wait and pray for their fulfillment, we tend to create images and expectations of what that fulfillment will look like. Yet when brought to completion, heaven's release of these things will often look different from our previously imagined outcomes. This is one good reason to hold our prophetic words *firmly* before the Lord in confident prayer, but *loosely* when forming perceptions of *when* or *how* we think they should play out!

Even before we had any outbuildings in place, the men who had come to live with us represented the small, instantaneous start of New Hope Ranch. They were *also* God's answer to help us build the fences. Good, old-fashioned work quiets the soul during the first weeks of sobriety, so Hal and the others gladly pitched right in. With coffee breaks to come in out of the snowy cold and a few extra community hands pitching in here and there, we were able to install the fence posts and string all the wire before our deadline of seven days had passed.

Our newest residents had food to eat and a warm, dry place to stay, and felt great about their contribution to the project. For our part, we were grateful that now Maggie and Pokey almost had a place to stay. I say *almost*, because we now had a fence, but no gate enclosures. Asking God about the next project for the ranch, He directed me with this word: "You need four gates that encircle the house, to set it apart as a tabernacle of meeting. The house is to be protected and separate from the ranch. You're not finished with the fences until you set the gates in place."

We had no money to buy gates. The purchase of the fencing materials had drained our finances and since I was still new at understanding God's supernatural supply, I took a walk along our dirt road, kicking up stones in frustration and wondering how in the world we could work out their purchase. Just then a silver-toned pick up headed my way and stopped by my side. The driver rolled down his window and asked, "Is this New Hope Ranch?" I answered with a nod and he continued. "I heard about you guys and, well, I have a little extra tithe money and I was wondering, is there anything you need?" My heart leaped into my throat and I answered honestly, "Yes sir, we need four gates to complete our fences."

Within three months of purchasing New Hope Ranch, the fences were completed with four gates surrounding our house, and Maggie and Pokey could now run freely within their corral. But more profound than the building of fences or gates was the work that happened in the hearts of our first four men. Each one successfully completed six months of detoxification and invited Jesus to be their Savior before heading off to build new lives. Tim and Willy, who had been running from the law, returned home to clear up their outstanding warrants. Hal moved to Colorado to begin a new life away from old influences and Devin was able to get a job locally and live a normal and productive life.

Anointing On Risk

Obedience almost always involves *risk*. Had Teresa and I decided to act according to our natural inclinations, we certainly would have chosen to stay in our well-paying jobs, living in the comfort of our home near the ocean, playing golf and experiencing a life of relative ease. Without risk, we would never have stepped out in obedience to pursue our vision. But counsel from other wise believers and the peace we sensed in our hearts were confirmation enough for us to see the ranch as God's direction for our lives.

> *As we move ahead step-by-step, we can usually sense whether our plans are God's plans by observing His anointing on our forward progress*

We've since learned to pay attention to the *favor of God* on our risks. *As we move ahead step-by-step, we can usually sense whether our plans are God's plans by observing His anointing on our forward progress.* God's *blessing* and *favor* on our steps gave us faith that we were 'on track' with Him and the encouragement we needed to move ahead. Favor came in the form of supernatural provisions, answered prayers and through finding support from people in the community. These things enabled trust that God's way was being established in our lives.

A word of clarification about hindrances that rise up when we risk: they don't necessarily mean God's not in a thing. Sometimes these roadblocks are a call for *redirection* and we only need to make a course correction in order to get back on track. Or, maybe our *timing* is wrong for plans we've initiated and we simply need to wait. The third possibility for understanding difficulties we experience is that the enemy could be creating some *harassment* to try and derail the work of the Kingdom, and we need the mind of God to know how to dismiss his interference. And finally, we may need to simply press toward God intently in prayer, to cry out for the breakthrough we are longing for.[24] If we're hitting obstacles, then the Spirit of wisdom will help us discern their source.[25] We only need to ask, and Father will clarify for us as we wait for His answer.

Divine Healing

After the gates were hung and our first four men had gone on to reenter society, we received another phone call. A twenty-

---

[24] *Micah 2:13, NIV*
[25] *Ephesians 1:17*

something alcoholic was being discharged from the hospital after a bout with pancreatitis and was already detoxing because of his hospital stay. Dallas asked if we could help him. We picked Jack up and brought him into our home, but by the next morning he was back in the hospital with another severe attack on his pancreas.

The doctors weren't certain he would live. I stood over his gurney in the emergency room and compassion for this lost young man washed over me. Pain wracked his body and fear clouded his soul. Laying hands on him, I prayed for the healing of his pancreas, then spoke kindly and wiped the hair from his face. "Jack, I love you and God loves you too. You're gonna' be okay and when you get well, call me and we'll come and get you and bring you out to the ranch."

Four days later, the phone rang and it was Jack. We met him at the hospital later that day and brought him back to the ranch, where he continued the program for a complete detoxification. After prayer and sobriety, his pancreas was healed and never bothered him again.

Added to the sobriety of Hal and the three hitchhikers, Jack's freedom from addiction was the beginning of more than a decade of liberating addicts and alcoholics by the discipling power of the Holy Spirit. Jack's physical healing also represented the first of many healings we would see in years to come.

A Good Start

We'd only begun. Barns and lean-tos, landscaping, horse stalls, a tack room and much more were still needed to make New Hope a working ranch where men could come and find release. Gradually stepping out in each new aspect of our venture, the Spirit's affirmations helped us understand the ranch wasn't just our dream, it was also *God's dream*, and He would continue walking with us to establish each step.[26] Lessons of risking with Him continued as we became more established, and the answers we received from heaven enlarged our capacity to believe God for greater and greater things.

Living a supernatural life has its challenges. Every single need we have is meant to be approached with confident trust in the *goodness* and *faithfulness* of Father God. But as directors of New Hope, reliance on God's moment-by-moment provision was often unsettling to our natural minds. Honestly, I don't want to ever relive some of our close-call situations! On the other hand, I wouldn't exchange for *any* earthly prize the faith we developed by watching God's miraculous supply and provision.

---

[26] *2 Corinthians 1:20-22*

For Further Reflection

1. Why do you think Rick and Teresa's dream of a recovery ranch took years to come into being? From what you've read so far in this book, what did you sense God was doing through their years of waiting? How did those years turn out to their benefit? Ask God to help you grasp what He's doing in your times of waiting for answered prayers and dreams to come true.

2. Have you ever received a prophetic word or a prophetic sign like the rainbow and birthday cake Rick and Teresa received? Ask God to increase your prophetic understanding. If you've never received a personal prophetic word, ask Him for one and wait patiently in assurance that He'll answer!

3. Why is it a good idea to hold loosely to the way we imagine our dreams will be fulfilled? On the other hand, why is it essential to continue to pray about our dreams?

4. Read about *obedient (listening) risk* in the lives of these people in the Bible: Paul, in Acts 16:9-15; Peter, in Matthew 14:25-31; the Israelites in 2 Chronicles 20:2-27. How did God anoint their steps and favor their willingness to risk in listening obedience? What was the result of their obedient risk?

5. How did Rick and Teresa keep their eyes on God in their present circumstances? How can living in the past, *or* living in the future, cause us to miss out on what God is doing *today*?

Prayer:

Father, thank You that Your heavenly plans for my life are fulfilled as we walk together, day by day. Shape all my dreams to agree with Your purposes in the spiritual realm. Help me risk in listening obedience, that I can experience Your favor and anointing. Take me by the hand and build in me the heart of a trusting child. Thank you, Papa God. Thank you, Jesus.

Hannah's Healing

At age four, a stranger molested Hannah.[27] Her mind blocked the memory of the trauma and as an adult, she only vaguely remembered a man carrying her away from her tricycle. That's where the impression stopped.

Hannah grew into an incredibly fearful adult. Afraid of being touched physically and afraid to say 'no' to anyone, Hannah lost her personality. Since she had no sense of personal boundaries, practically everyone could impose their will upon hers.

Hannah went for therapy to deal with her fears and was raped by her therapist. When it was discovered he had done the same to four other innocent women, this devious perpetrator lost his license. But for Hannah, the damage done through further trauma only served to cement her internal fears.

She married, and as the daughter of a good Southern Baptist pastor, intended to stay married for life. Her husband made a great income, they were well off financially and on the outside, seemed like the perfect couple. But behind closed doors their home often carried cycles of abuse. Hannah learned to put on a fake smile and pretend everything was okay. She was a survivor.

---

[27] *not her real name*

Stumbling Into Healing

After eight years, the marriage finally began falling apart because of multiple affairs. During that time, Hannah stumbled into a relationship with Teresa, Rick and New Hope's family of believers. The ranch atmosphere became a thread of hope and Hannah spent more and more time hanging around during meals, meetings and just about any other time people were at home.

Seeing the miracles that happened on a regular basis at the ranch stirred something in Hannah's heart. She knew Jesus, but He was something of an *emergency-prayer-only* kind of God. Yet, the people at the ranch seemed to depend on Him for *everything*: food, provisions, personal items, and more. And God actually *answered* their prayers, including healing many of the men and women who had lived addictive lifestyles!

Teresa kept telling Hannah she needed to forgive her ex- husband. Slowly, she was able to release him from every offense. Her husband eventually apologized for his sins against her, further releasing Hannah's heart from remaining ties of bitterness and unforgiveness.

More internal freedom came as God removed the guilt she carried over committing a teenage abortion. She had been able to forgive herself, but since Hannah had killed her own child in the womb, she assumed God could never use her to minister to others.

Then one evening, God showed her two people in the Bible who had killed someone, yet were used by God. Moses, who killed a man, led the Israelites out of Egypt. And Saul (later called Paul), before meeting Jesus on the road to Damascus, hauled many Christians off to prison and certain death. Paul went on to establish many of the early New Testament churches.

Hannah realized if God used Moses and Paul, He *could* use her after all! She began to minister to other women who had abortions, bringing hope and forgiveness to their lives. She was becoming a part of the family at New Hope, sharing love and honor, offering her gifts and receiving from others.

One evening Teresa invited women to gather together for a time of ministry and healing concerning sexual issues. Hannah decided to attend, even though she didn't think she had any sexual issues. She just went to socialize with the other ladies who were at the meeting.

At one point Teresa invited the women, "I want you to remember when you quit dancing as a little girl: what happened when you were young, to stop that?" Suddenly, the image of the man who carried her away from her tricycle at the age of four flooded her mind, but this time the memory expanded. Hannah saw the whole scene unfolding before her eyes: the shed, the molestation, the horror of it all. In a safe environment, God unveiled the deep root of her fears and through ministry she received that night, she was set free from her prison.

Hannah is no longer co-dependent. People don't walk all over her, and neither is she a captive to fear and depression. She has begun to know who she is as a child of God and how she fits in His family. By now, Hannah's seen plenty of her own miracles of provision and supernatural healings.

She currently ministers to women who have experienced the pain of divorce, abortion and more. Her own experiences have given her compassion and her relationship with the Holy Spirit enables her to lead them tenderly towards the same Healer who so lovingly and faithfully set her free.

5

THE GOD OF MORE

The ranch's propane tank was empty and we had no heat, hot water or gas for cooking. With ten men in our recovery program, something had to be done about the fact that we were all taking cold showers and burning scrap wood in the barbeque grill to make our meals.

Selling Whalen and Willie at the livestock auction seemed to be our only option for immediate cash. Now full grown cows, as calves we'd bottle-fed them almost from birth. They had become tame and playful like pets and letting go of them wasn't going to be easy.

On the way home from the auction, I tried to hide my tears from the rest of those riding along in the truck. Wondering why in the world we hadn't seen God provide in a different way, Teresa and I were both upset. I'd had it in my heart to build a herd of cattle and letting go of our only two cows made no sense to my natural understanding. To make matters worse, Whalen and Willie, along with nine baby goats we'd sold from our goatherd, had gone for much less on the auction block than I'd expected. I was tremendously discouraged.

While I was attempting to hide my tears, Teresa quietly asked God why we had to get rid of the cows. Graciously, the Holy Spirit answered her with this promise: *"Because you've been obedient to sell your cows, I'll give you **more** cows."* Heaven's response to our willingness to surrender was the promise of *more.* We knew we'd chosen to take Whalen and Willie to auction for the sake of providing for our men. Since we were willing to sacrifice, God promised to bring us through this trial to a place of even greater blessing.

> **Heaven's response to our willingness to surrender was the promise of more**

Still grumbling slightly in my heart, we returned home to a heated house and hot water. While we'd been away at auction, a local resident had donated a partial tank of propane and with additional cash in our pockets to top off the tank, we could breathe more easily. We were sad, but at least everyone was warm and nourished.

Two days later, Aaron Williams called. Aaron is a neighbor of Bob Smith, one of New Hope's board members. Bob and his wife Molly owned a large working ranch and mentored us in the ins and outs of running our smaller ranch. One day each week, we took the men over to their place to help with just about any kind of work that facilitated managing a cattle ranch: moving and branding cows, assisting during vaccinations, pulling weeds, construction of buildings and much more. The work was good medicine for the men's souls and in an informal exchange for helping, our residents usually received personal ministry from the Smiths, from Aaron and from Don Lamay, who also lived nearby. All were strong believers and loved to encourage others.

On the other end of the phone line Aaron asked, "Rick, we've been praying about helping you start a herd of cattle: would it be alright if we bring you some cows?" Remembering the Holy Spirit's promise to Teresa on our ride home from selling Whalen and Willie, I was amazed at God's fast response and accepted Aaron's offer gratefully. A few hours later, a trailer arrived at our ranch and five pregnant, long-eared Brahma and Angus mixed heifers, all uniform in size, were unloaded into our corral.

Starting a cattle herd with cows that are the same size is important so that when reproduction occurs, the bone structure of the calves will be strong and healthy. Our new cows were even in height and they were all registered stock. As Aaron and Don pulled away, we marveled at our new herd of five, soon to double to ten with the birth of their calves. The men in the program joyfully picked out names for our new bovine residents and began to happily bond with their unique personalities.

As though God were sealing His promise by pouring out even *more* blessing, within a few days, three additional cows were donated to our ranch. A registered Beefmaster bull, worth about $3000.00, came from Aaron's stock. Another heifer arrived as a gift from Bob and Molly, and Gallagher Livestock in Fallon, Nevada, brought us a cow the men named *Katie*.

Beyond Sacrifice

God had kept His promise. After our personal sacrifice, He'd given us *more!* We were beginning to discover this was simply

> **God always puts something better beyond the point of our sacrifice**

part of His nature: **God always puts something better beyond the point of our sacrifice.** Releasing Whalen and Willie was hard, but our willingness to let them go brought us to a greater level of maturity and trust, where we could then *receive* **more** *blessing.* In our case, the 'more' was a herd of thirteen!

James writes in the Bible that trials have a purpose. They're not to be a source of discouragement or fear. The spiritual reality is, as we trust God in the middle of a trial, we develop *patience* so that *we won't lack anything:*

> "Consider it pure joy...whenever you face trials of many kinds, because you know that the testing of your faith develops patience. Patience must finish its work so that you may be *mature and complete,* not *lacking anything." James 1:2-4 (NIV/NKJV)*

Patience develops *maturity* and maturity releases *blessing.* The patience of walking through a challenge helps us grow up and our maturity is what enables us to then *receive more* from our royal Father, who doesn't want us to lack anything!

As Christians we're already heirs of God in the realm of the Spirit. We rule and reign with Him.[28] But there are levels of being entrusted with more as we grow in our Christian lives. In an earthly kingdom, a nine-year-old reigning heir will be given less authority than a thirty-year-old reigning heir. The principle is the same in the kingdom of heaven, where the process of spiritual growth shapes our character and increases our authority as heirs who rule with Father.

When I had to let go of hopes for building a herd with Whalen and Willie, God allowed the circumstances to develop my trust and character. Was I willing to give up my own desires in order to serve others? Could I love the men in our program, even if it meant surrendering the idea of growing our herd? Did I believe God was good in the midst of it all? The Father answered my obedient trust with an increase of *provision* and *responsibility*.

The end result of all we go through on this earth is that we receive a wonderful **crown** of life for enduring. James 1:12 *(NIV)* says, *Blessed is the man who perseveres under trial, because when he has stood the test, he will receive the* crown of life *that God has promised to those who love him.* God's reward for His children is always better than anything we'll ever sacrifice or surrender. As heirs of God, there's a blessing beyond everything we experience in this earth. He can take every pain

---

[28] *Romans 8:17*

Turn our painful experiences to blessing

and every difficulty of our lives and in time, turn these experiences to blessings!

Challenges Mean God's Solutions

Along with our horses and goats, we were thrilled to have a herd of cattle at the ranch. A week or so after they arrived on the property, I figured we were getting low on our hay supply and walked over to our stack yard to find out exactly where we stood in terms of feed for the animals. Three lonely bales remained. That meant we had about a day's worth of feed. Indeed, the Holy Spirit had been true to His word and blessed us with more cows, but we were still financially strapped and at the moment, buying hay was impossible without divine intervention.

Walking outside, I began to pray in the spirit and soon found myself on my hands and knees at the bottom of our corrals. Praying for quite awhile, I'd lost awareness of my surroundings and when I came to my senses, a great peace washed over my soul. The Spirit of God reminded me of God's audible word, spoken to me as a young believer: "*My Son, when you know these things come from Me, all things will be added to you.*" Responding with all my heart, I offered God full surrender. "God, whatever you want me to do; if you want me to sell the herd and the horses, I'll do it; If you want me to train these men without the animals, I'll do it; Whatever you want, God, I'll follow you."

Though I was serious about my commitment, the promise I'd just made was no small thing and I returned to the house to read and encourage myself in the Word. Twenty minutes later, the phone rang. "Hi, Rick, I just got a good deal on four hundred bales of hay, so I bought them for your ranch. You'll need to pick them up and weigh them, since I bought them by the ton. Would you be able to take care of that for me?" Aaron Williams was God's answer once again. Thrilled and delighted, I thanked him and the men joined me in picking up a generous, three-month supply of hay bales for our animals!

> **When God puts a challenge in front of us, he also puts the solution in front of us**

In the midst of our desperate needs, we were experiencing the Father's timely and specific answers. Each miraculous response wrote on our hearts the tremendous testimony of His faithfulness. Slowly, fears of lack, abandonment and failure we'd learned in our former lives were being washed away. We began to grasp the simple truth that *when God puts a challenge in front of us, he also puts the solution in front of us.* Rather than looking at the desperation of a problem, we were learning to look *through* the problem to anticipate heaven's solutions. Problems were becoming a gateway to kingdom miracles.

Developing A Testimony

Bill Johnson, a well-known Christian leader who trains the present-day church in experiencing the supernatural, explains that in the context of Revelations 19:10, *testimony* about what

God's already done will release His presence to do it again! If God could provide us with herds and hay, we could also watch Him heal and save and deliver. We began to pray more boldly.

Over and over again, as our ranch was established we saw God supernaturally meet every need. Telephone poles were given to build additional corrals. Railroad ties came for constructing paddocks. Free wood from glass crates provided boards for the small animals barn, and one of our men announced he'd become a 'believer in Jesus' when a whole truckload of reclaimed lumber arrived the morning after he prayed for enough boards to finish the barn for the horses.

Red Shoes

We learned to pray about *everything*, including our own personal needs and desires.[29] During this season, Teresa was tired of her minimal wardrobe. She sighed and shuffled through her clothing absentmindedly. Toward the back of the closet, she noticed a beautiful red dress she'd not worn much because she had no appropriate, matching shoes. Now a man's response to this kind of clothing dilemma would have been to just wear what he has, without giving it another thought. But a woman needs to feel like she's a princess, so shoes that match an outfit are important!

Teresa talked to God about her desire. "Lord, I have no shoes to go with this red dress. Would you please provide me with red shoes that will match?" The next morning, the doorbell

---

[29] *Philippians 4:6*

rang and one of the men answered the door. Someone was donating a bag of clothing items toward our ranch's upcoming yard sale fundraiser. Later as Teresa sorted through the bag, she pulled out three beautiful pairs of red shoes that just happened to be her size. One pair had tall heels, a second pair had shorter heels, and the third was a pair of flats. Teresa laughed and praised God, sensing that because she hadn't been specific with her request, God had abundantly provided her with several options!

Meat Of The Matter

Another time, we'd run out of meat. Seated together at the evening dinner table, we all bowed our heads and humbly asked God to provide meat for our household. While we were still passing family-style bowls of food around the table during the meal, a gentleman interrupted us by knocking on our dining room's sliding glass doors. He held several large metal trays in his hands, filled with a variety of frozen meats. "I've just emptied my freezer and I've got all this meat," he said. "I was wondering, do you want it?" Jaws dropped open in amazement, all around the table, at how quickly the Lord had answered our request!

Trees For Landscaping

The land around the ranch compound was still bare, gray earth and we desperately wanted trees for beauty. But even more importantly, trees would provide needed shade relief from the scorching desert sun. After making our request to Father God during our corporate prayer times with the men, a whole supply of large saplings came our way from a local school organization's unwanted surplus.

No Need Too Small

No need was beyond of the reach of our prayers. We asked for toilet paper and someone knocked on the door and stood there offering us supply of toilet paper. Teresa asked God for nylons and Molly Smith stopped by to visit. In the course of their conversation Molly casually handed Teresa a pair of nylons. "I don't know why, but I bought these for you," she commented. Teresa thanked her and gratefully explained she'd been praying for nylons!

Accidentally Saddled

Some of God's answers came through rather unusual circumstances, like our need for more saddles, bridles and miscellaneous riding tack. We had several horses but only one old saddle, and that meant the men had to take turns riding. When we prayed for saddles and all the other things we'd need to outfit all our horses, a series of strange circumstances brought not only the tack, but *also* a larger horse trailer.

One of our men was returning from nearby Fallon, pulling the horse trailer behind our pick up, when a young driver accidentally hit him from behind. No one was harmed, but the insurance company deemed our trailer a total loss.

With a $1,700.00 settlement check in hand, I began looking for a replacement. As I discussed the matter with the Lord I heard Him say, "Go into Carson City and you'll find a horse trailer for sale." On the drive back from Reno a few days later, I obeyed the Holy Spirit and drove through Carson City, rather than taking my usual route home. Sure enough, a used five-stall horse trailer sat on a car lot in the middle of the city. "Lord, we can't afford that!" I argued with small faith, knowing the trailer was worth far more than we could possibly swing financially. But the Spirit's impression remained, "Rick, go back and look at that trailer."

I approached the sales desk at the used car lot without any confidence. "I'm Rick McKinney, from New Hope Recovery Ranch and we need a horse trailer, but I'm sure that one costs at least $5,000.00 and we only have $1,700.00. I imagine you probably don't want to sell it to me, but God told me to come and ask about it." I was really doubtful, so much so, that I started to turn around and walk out the door before I heard a response.

"Wait a minute!" The sales person called after me. "Let me call the owner of the trailer and find out how much he'll accept as a purchase price." Forty-five minutes later, the seller arrived and we shook hands. "My wife and I are believers" he said, "and our kids are grown, so we're selling the horses. We've heard about your recovery ranch. I was thinking I'd like to have at least $1,800.00 for the trailer. How much money do you have?"

By making a few phone calls, I was able to come up with the extra cash needed for the purchase and we agreed to meet later in the day to finalize the sale. That afternoon when the owner and his wife met us, *a whole supply of tack* lay near the trailer. "Listen, Rick, we're going to throw in our riding tack for free. We don't need it anymore so it's yours if you can use it." Looking over their gear, I realized absolutely everything we'd prayed for was there: two saddles, bridles, bits and more. Absolutely free.

Only God could take a negative circumstance like the accident and through prayer, turn it around to orchestrate His good in our lives. The tack we received, worth about $3,000.00, outfitted all our ranch horses and the new trailer, worth much more than the amount of the insurance settlement check, was a great upgrade for the ranch.

Houses And Lands

Only humans tend to think God has a harder time providing larger gifts, but Jesus doesn't see answered prayer in terms of size or difficulty. We'd been going to the local women's prison once a week to minister to women inmates and Teresa really wanted to expand New Hope to include a ministry for ladies. When our neighbor placed her ranch home on the real estate market, Teresa and I began praying for a way to buy it as home for women.

After our neighbor's property had been listed for quite some time, our friends from California, Al and Sue Kuhn, came to stay with us for a few days. During the course of conversation we shared with them about our desire to add a home for women to New Hope's facilities.

The next day, all four of us were standing outside and praying together in a circle, when Al looked over at the neighbor's house. "Is that property for sale?" he asked out of the blue. We nodded and he added, "I think the Lord told me I'm supposed to buy it for you. Why don't you check out the selling price?" At that very moment Robyn, the owner of the house, drove up to greet us. We asked about the house and she explained that it had been off the market for a few months, but was being listed for sale again the following week.

When our friends returned home, Al wrote us a check to cover the entire purchase of the property and New Hope had a women's home. Nothing is too hard for heaven's generous supply!

The God Of More

Walking through trials with patience demonstrates we're willing to trust God is a *good* Father who *rewards* our faith.[30] We know our character is maturing when we can actually be joyful in the middle of a challenge. Joy is evidence that we *believe* God, who promises we won't lack any good thing.[31]

Since God's solutions can come to us in a way or a time frame we're not expecting, we need perseverance and flexibility. Some provisions are immediate, like the meat that showed up on our doorstep only minutes after we'd prayed around the

---

[30] *Hebrews 11:6*
[31] *Psalm 34:10; Psalm 84:11*

dinner table. Others require patience, like praying consistently for a woman's ministry house and many months later, receiving the neighbor's ranch home. Lots of answers will arrive unconventionally, like the boards for the barn that came to us in the form of glass crates that needed to be pulled apart, or the riding tack that showed up as part of a vehicle insurance settlement.

The Bible speaks of God's ways as much higher than ours.[32] As His children, we'll never completely understand why He answers in particular manner or in certain time frames that may not fit our own perspectives. Whatever form God's answers take, the point of the provision is that He is growing our trust in His nature as our generous Father and Brother. When the Holy Spirit answers our prayers, each provision is meant to establish our faith in God's goodness. And if we're willing to risk with Him, He will consistently take us to new levels of maturity, so that He can continue to give us more. He is always a *good* God who gives increase to His children.

Spend Some time Praying in the Spirit ♡

---

[32] *Isaiah 55:9*

Praying in the Spirit

For Further Reflection

1. What challenges in your life need God's solutions? Spend some time praying in the Spirit over these needs. Pour them out to the Father in prayer, releasing all from your own hands and placing them in His. Be patient as God moves heaven and earth to bring His solutions. If you like, share your needs with another believer and pray about them together.

2. Do you have a testimony of answered prayer? Testimonies demonstrate that what God has already done, He can *do again*. Start a journal to record God's supernatural activity in your life. Recording His answers reminds you of His faithfulness in the past and builds trust for even greater things in your future. In five or ten years, you'll be amazed as you read your own testimonies of God's goodness!

3. Where is your patience being tested? In what areas are you being matured? Ask God to show you what He's doing in your life through your trial and as His royal heir, how He desires to grow your character so you can receive *more*.

4. How has your understanding of personal *sacrifice* changed as a result of reading this chapter? Take a few days to read the Bible's story of Joseph's years in prison and his eventual rule in Egypt (Genesis 37-46). As you read, ask God to show you throughout the story, how Joseph's years of testing were used to build and change his character, so he could then receive *more*. Take note of the end result of his years of trial, not only for his own life, but also for his family and the nation of Egypt.

Prayer:

Father, I am beginning to realize the value system of Your spiritual realm is much greater than earthly mindsets. Please open my spiritual eyes to see from your point of view. Open my spiritual ears to hear your direction and guidance. Help me to trust, to enjoy obedient, listening risk and to see your way for my life. Build trust in my heart, one day at a time. Please touch the areas of my soul where my trust has been broken and restore the hope and joy of walking hand in hand with You as Your child. Thank You that You always hear me, and You're faithful to answer.

Meet Max

You would think being raised in a church and having a wonderful grandmother and mother to support me as I grew up would be enough to guide me toward a quality life. But before Mom and Dad divorced, arguments filled the atmosphere of our home and sometimes their fights ended in physical abuse. Lack of affection and family violence created a deep pain in my young heart. That ache never went away and eventually caused me to tumble headlong into the numbing world of addictions.

Grandmother, who lived with Mom and me, was the only adult I fully trusted with my love and when she died, I felt completely alone. Without her support I started drinking, desperate to escape feelings of loneliness, inadequacy and self-loathing that gnawed at my soul. I often stole bottles of booze and cigarettes from the grocery store where I worked as a teenager and hid in our basement to drink, until drunkenness covered my internal unhappiness and brought a twisted kind of relief.

Though I was tremendously popular in high school, none of my peers realized I wrestled with a constant fear of rejection. When my drinking started to interfere with being a star athlete I switched to marijuana, until an injured knee took me out of all sports competition and I was no longer able to identify myself as a 'jock'. Needing another persona that would keep me popular, I decided to become a perpetual partygoer. That I could drink longer and harder than anyone else was a real source of personal pride. At all-night parties, I was the one who woke up the next morning and finished off all the half empty drinks still littering the room.

For a while, using drugs turned into selling, particularly cocaine, but soon I returned to alcohol as my mainstay and consumed a fifth each day. That's the equivalent of 25.6 shots, or 750 *ml* flowing into my system on a daily basis. No one wanted to be around a drunk who passed out on them: friends, family and even my girlfriend left, because I'd become an embarrassment and a thief who stole from them in order to support my addictions.

Coming to New Hope
Homeless at age twenty-four and hauled to jail repeatedly for theft or drunkenness, I heard about *New Hope Recovery Ranch* through a church I attended during occasional days of lucidity. After numerous attempts on my own to quit alcohol, and even sticking out two months at a different recovery program, I decided to try New Hope.

I consider my time at the ranch to be the *beginning of my life.* Immersed into an environment that helped me start a relationship with Jesus and with the Holy Spirit, Christianity became real. I'd always believed, but now the truths were becoming personal. I was *experiencing* Jesus, not just hearing about Him.

Developing a new work ethic was crucial. During school and

every job I'd ever had, I did the least amount of work I could, in order to 'get by'. At New Hope, we learned how to be responsible and diligent on a daily basis and how to take pride in our work, something I'd never learned as a child or a teenager. The change of attitude was refreshing and gave me new focus.

Aside from meeting God personally, the greatest impact came when we began to examine our lives through the lens of The Twelve Steps and Spiritual Disciplines[33]. Steps four through six were most significant to me:

4. *Made a searching and fearless moral inventory of ourselves.*
5. *Admitted to God, to ourselves and to another human being the exact nature of our wrongs.*
6. *Were entirely ready to have God remove all these defects of character.*
7. *Humbly asked Him to remove our shortcomings.*

When I realized God could completely *remove* from my heart all the sins I'd committed against many, many people, a thousand pound weight rolled off my shoulders and I became light as a feather. Every terrible thing I had ever done was forgiven through Jesus' blood!

Fear of rejection lost its power as I received God's love and learned to love myself. No longer guilty and ashamed, I spoke about my life with a transparency that was entirely new. As a

---

[33] *Copyright information on The Twelve Steps and Spiritual Disciplines is listed at the front of the book.*

user, I'd learned to lie as easily as breathing, but now I wanted to be honest and truthful.

Sober for eighteen months, I've successfully completed the program at New Hope. When I arrived at the ranch I carried two duffle bags and a pillow. When I left, I carried Jesus and the Holy Spirit in my heart. I was clean and free.

Slowly, restoration is taking place with family members and former friends. Though I thought our relationships were finished, God has been rebuilding what was lost. He's also given me a whole new spiritual family in my hometown of Jackson, Nevada, and I now have hope and love as the basis for all my friendships.

I've begun college classes for my career, but more importantly I have a greater purpose in life, something I'd been looking for all those years while partying as a teenager and a young adult. Wrapped up in these promises is my true goal, and no one can ever take it from me:

And so we know and rely on the love God has for us. God is love. Whoever lives in love lives in God, and God in him. In this way, love is made complete among us so that we will have confidence on the day of judgment, because in this world we are like him. (1 John 4:16,17, NIV)

6

PRIORITY: RELATIONSHIPS

Relationship Or Activity?

At the end of two years of cattle herding I stood on top of a high desert hill, with the herd grazing all around me. The brilliant sun beautifully accentuated hues of earthy reds, whites, grays and browns that stretched out in the valley below, as far the eye could see. In that quiet grandeur God came to me with the same query He'd made once before, a few months prior: "Rick, what do you want to do, raise cows or preach?"

New Hope Recovery Ranch was absolutely buzzing with activity. Our herd had grown sizably and for the last two years we'd run it on 730 acres of irrigated pastureland. Men at the ranch grew in manhood through daily ranching routines and found healing through a weekly twelve-step program called

Celebrate Recovery. Regular guest speakers and worship teams brought spiritual growth, and Sunday mornings rounded out our corporate life together.

We started seeing healings and deliverance from demonic bondages at the ranch. Local believers heard about the good things God was doing and they showed up to join us. Soon more than one hundred people were coming to receive impartation from guest speakers or to experience healing prayer, inner healing and deliverance. A small church fellowship blossomed naturally at New Hope and now, in addition to our recovery ministry we were also pastoring a church.

By this point in our venture, working with the cattle required quite a bit of time and as I thought about all the activities Teresa and I had become involve in, I realized I was no longer being effective in much of anything in my life. I could continue to run the herd, minister to the men and women in the program and carry out all my other responsibilities, but nothing would be done with *excellence.*

While communing with God high on the hill that day, He posed to me a second question, "Rick, whom do you want to serve?" Of course, for me there was only one answer. "Lord, I want to serve You!" Lovingly but firmly God responded, "Then you need to make a decision".

Divine Shift

Once again, things were about to shift in my life. Every time God redirected me it was always for my own good, but that didn't necessarily make the changes any easier to face. God's questions to me that day presented a choice: *relationships* or a life of cattle herding. The time and effort required for running the herd was taking away from my involvement in the lives of people.

I'm firmly convinced if my answer to Him had been that I wanted to keep the herd and dismantle New Hope's Recovery ministry, God would have blessed me. Our fellowship on top of windy desert hills among grazing cattle would have continued to bring us both joy, whether or not I ever ministered again. But I wanted to honor God's heart in the matter and I knew He loved people deeply, especially the broken, the bruised and the captive.

> *His answers satisfied my fear of releasing the present in order to embrace the future*

I made the difficult decision to take the cows to the livestock auction. Running the cattle herd had been the fulfillment of a personal dream and letting go was hard, so I pressed into God with the burden I felt. His answers satisfied my fear of releasing the *present* in order to embrace the *future*.

I saw in the next phase, after the cattle were gone, the ranch would become more like a school of His Spirit. Prodigals, like the one in Jesus' famous parable, would come: they would be spiritually hungry men who were ready to receive the Holy Spirit and then move on in their lives.[34]

---

[34] *Luke 15:11-32*

Sure enough, after the sale of our herd, the spiritual boundaries of the ranch exploded. The whole emphasis of daily activities changed, centering more on training and teaching, and less on ranch work. We still had the horses, goats and other smaller animals to give our residents stimulating animal interaction and help in developing healthy life disciplines. But all of that now came in smaller doses. In addition to allowing more spiritual input, the extra time in the men's schedules also enabled them to be more involved in the lives of people in our growing community of local believers.

Relationship Or Ministry?

The change of direction from *activity* to *relationship* was God's first course correction to steer my life toward prioritizing people. Another and more serious course correction was looming on the horizon and this one was much harder. Had I missed it, my marriage may have been destroyed.

> The change of direction from **activity** to relationship **was** God's first course correction to steer my life toward prioritizing people

At the beginning of the ranch, when the first four men showed up on our doorstep, we took them into our own home. There simply was no other option, no other place for them to live. Since we had carried the dream of the recovery ranch in our hearts for so many years, we were willing to lay aside our own needs for privacy. Ministering to the men made us feel completely alive and we thrived on seeing God change their lives.

But after four and a half years of sharing a house with twelve male recovering alcoholics and drug addicts, my marital 'garden' with Teresa had become overrun with weeds and varmints. She often hid in our bedroom, feeling absolutely overwhelmed by being surrounded with so many needy people, especially since she was the only woman!

In my ignorance I just kept moving forward, but finally Teresa had enough. She could no longer live with her house full of recovering addicts, and left to spend some time in a friend's cabin. God had spoken to her, "Teresa, come away with me," and she answered Him by packing her bags and moving out, not knowing whether she could ever return to our present living situation. We both thought our marriage was over.

My heart was broken. I'd lost the woman I loved because of ministry, but I couldn't envision throwing twelve men out on the street in order to win her back. Desperately, I sought counsel from other leaders. Every word I received was the same: continue serving the men, continue pastoring the people in the fellowship, and let God do His work in the situation between Teresa and myself.

I carried on with ministry, but inside I was dying. Finally I invited Dave Hollister, an evangelist, to come and speak at the ranch. When the two of us were alone I poured out my heart and asked for his advice. He laid his hand on my shoulder and after listening for wisdom from the Holy Spirit, shared what he was hearing "Rick, you need to pursue your wife. She needs to know she is more important to you than ministry."

His words were a confirmation of what I sensed in my spirit. Gathering the men in the program around our dining room table, I explained that for the sake of our marriage they needed to find another place to live. I gave them a few days to make other living arrangements and then went to share with Teresa that I was not willing to lose her: whatever I had to do, even closing down the ministry, I would do in order for us to come together again.

Divine Ingenuity

The day after announcing to the men they needed to move out, someone happened to call the ranch to offer us a free, used travel trailer. Several hours later, a second caller donated an airstream trailer. The following day two more people phoned, each one giving the ranch a small mobile home and by the end of that same day, one more person had phoned to donate another travel trailer.

I figured God was up to something! During two days and without any solicitation, five people had independently and spontaneously given us various small trailers. Father God was concerned about the men's welfare and almost humorously decided to provide temporary solutions for their living situations at the ranch. I marveled at God's ingenuity.

Over the few months that Teresa had pulled away to be alone, her relationship with Jesus had been rekindled from a dying ember into a burning flame. When I promised her I would place our marriage above all else and backed my commitment by preparing a house where only the two of us would live, Teresa knew the time had come for her to move home.

With Teresa's full blessing, we moved the men into the ministry house where all the women had been staying and moved the women into the five travel trailers with their children, sisters and friends. Everyone had a place to stay, but most importantly, Teresa and I could now start learning the art of making marriage and relationship the first priority of our life.

Ministry Home

I shared in chapter four that we often sense whether our plans are God's plans by observing His anointing on our forward progress. Shortly after the temporary housing solution came by way of the five trailer donations, I noticed a manufactured home in an empty lot that needed a tremendous amount of work. Even so, the trailer held potential for a permanent, second ministry home at New Hope, and offered a possible solution for effectively housing all our residents.

After the owner gave us the run-down trailer, we towed it onto our property. Needing practically everything - new flooring, new roof, new plumbing, windows - we watched as, step-by-step the old trailer turned into a cozy home through the kindness and generosity of our greater community of relationships.

One afternoon I followed a nudge to stop in at Northern Nevada Supply, a plumbing supply company. God had whispered, "Go see Tom Rehiglio at 2:00 PM." I dropped what I was doing and drove to his offices in Reno. Tom was the head of the supply company and though we'd never met, he made time for me. He knew about New Hope because his daily commute took him right by our property.

Tom asked what I'd come to talk about. After explaining about the trailer I answered, "I need a septic tank, Tom". He responded, "Sounds like you need more than that!" I agreed and nodded my head as he continued, "You don't have any pipe, do you?" I said we didn't and Tom pushed back his chair. "Alright, I'm going to set up an account at our desk. Whatever you need, just come and sign for it. I'll take care of you. You'll need conduit, boxes, plumbing, sinks, toilets, leech lines. You come and get it." By the time we'd finished our meeting, I was crying in amazement at Tom's generosity and God's goodness.

Northern Nevada Supply had just donated thousands of dollars to New Hope and their aid was only the first of a series of donations that followed. Another couple that had once visited our fellowship later arrived with all the supplies for a new sheet-rock roof. They stayed at the ranch, laid the roof and also wrapped the windows. Someone else donated and installed flooring and carpet. Several helped to decorate. Even the men got into the act, building bunk beds and painting the interior walls.

In a matter of months New Hope had two great ministry homes, one for men and one for women. And equally as important, Teresa and I had our own home as a refuge where we could cultivate intimacy and love in our marriage.

To Love, being loved & give Love

Foundations Of Life And Ministry

We are made for *relationship*. It is the center, the highest aim of life. Our primary destiny is not to have a ministry or to be an effective witness, or even to walk in great power and anointing. And while God certainly wants us to know our purpose, even that is not His main goal for our life. His goal is that we become really good at *being loved* and at *giving love*. All of life is to flow out of relationship.[35]

If we want to be like Jesus, we'll always live in the context of relationship. He ministered to the masses, but often pulled away to be with smaller groups of covenant friends and in particular, with His twelve disciples. Among those twelve men, He had deeper times of intimacy with only three, Peter, James and John. Jesus' example of varying levels of friendships is an excellent pattern for us to follow.

> *We are made for relationship. It is the center; the highest aim of life*

The Lord shared everything with the disciples, whom He called His true friends.[36] Jesus always spoke openly and truthfully to His disciples with integrity and love. Like Him, we need friends who will speak into our lives and call us to greater levels of faith and Kingdom growth. These covenant friends should be those with whom we can be open, transparent and real, able to communicate all the strengths and weaknesses in our hearts.

---

[35] *1 Corinthians 13:1-8; Mark 12:30,31*
[36] *John 15:15*

123

These relationships are part of the 'guidance system' of the Holy Spirit. Some people in our lives are mentors, like my AA sponsor, Richard Pelletier, who gave spiritual sustenance to my first days as a newly recommitted believer. Kay Peterson was another example of a friend God used to help direct us to lay down our jobs and embrace the beginning of the ranch.

Other positive relationships in Jesus' life were people He'd healed, who then became followers and even supported Him financially as He travelled. His greater circle of friends included Lazarus and his two sisters, Martha and Mary, who are famous for their honest interactions with the Lord; Mary Magdalene; and even influential citizens of the time.[37]

Without relationships, we could not operate New Hope Ranch. Besides love and personal encouragement of close friends, many others have contributed to the growth of the ranch in practical ways. From donating supplies or monthly support, to helping train and teach the program participants, we have seen that our relationships with people all across America have been used by God to bless our residents and provide for their needs. New Hope has certainly been a 'group effort'!

Teresa and I are still learning to prioritize life according to relationships and we're especially learning to guard our marriage and make it the most important part of our lives. It's not easy, but the fruit of protecting and nurturing our love is this: life has become fun and ministering together has been a tremendous joy. Ministry from relationship really *is* all it's

---

[37] *Luke 8:2,3*

'cracked up to be'. I wouldn't trade it for all the cattle herds west of the Mississippi!

For Further Reflection

1. Are there any **activities** in your life that you sense may be hindering your relationships with people or with God? Ask God for wisdom, discernment and understanding about how you spend your time. In the same way that New Hope's cattle herd had to go, if there *is* an activity in your life that is draining relationships, ask God for help in knowing what action(s) you need to take, to reorder your life. You may even want to seek counsel about your schedule and priorities.

2. What have other people **unselfishly given** into your life? Where have you **generously given** into the lives of others? When has giving demonstrated the kind heart of God to you? How does giving with a free and liberal heart change other people? How has it changed you?

3. What **relationships** are **priorities** in your life? Are these friendships nurturing? Do they build up your identity in Jesus and strengthen your understanding of the King and the kingdom of God? Are you the kind of friend who builds up your friends and encourages them? If you're married, is your marriage *the* priority in all your earthly relationships? If the answer to any of these questions is 'no', you may want to consider God's heart for you, for your marriage and for your friendships. He has a way to heal us and even our spouse and

125

our friends, so that our relationships can be healthy and strong. Ask for counsel from wise and mature believers, who can help you grow and develop in patterns of healthy inter-personal relationships.

Prayer:

Jesus, I'd love to grow in my friendship with You. Show me how to see, sense, feel, and hear Your voice. Teach me to recognize when Your presence is near. Holy Spirit, help my spirit to know when You draw close. And if there's anything standing between us, show me what to do in order to be able to be closer to You. I want to walk and talk with You often!

As for my earthly relationships, help me to be at rest with my friends, and to give and receive love as a healthy and maturing friend. Show me what godly intimacy looks like with close friends. Teach me what it means to be real and open and trust-ing. Protect me from unwise friendships, and bring the right friends into my life. Thanks, big Brother, my King. I love You.

Debra's Journey

In 2001, I was fighting a losing battle against alcohol. Teresa McKinney promised to help, giving me her word that my life would change. That promise became my lifeline. From the time I'd started drinking as a teenager, I never remembered anyone presenting me with a hopeful outlook on my future.

Teresa shared her testimony with me: how broken she'd once been, but then Jesus met her as the love she'd been searching for her entire life. I wept at hearing her story and when she asked if I wanted to invite Jesus to rescue and save me, I eagerly said *yes!*

His presence came into me with an incredible peace that took away a mountain of anxiety I'd been feeling about difficult situations existing in my family. Soaking in everything I possibly could, I became like a spiritual sponge at our twelve step meetings, at church and in my personal times with Teresa.

I quickly learned alcohol was not the source of my personal struggles. Drinking was merely a bandage that covered up festering wounds of unforgiveness, anger, fear and deep personal pain. Everything had to change: my foul language, my stubborn independence, my selfishness, and all my unforgiveness. Thankfully, God was in me to wash away the old as His Spirit gave me the desire to do things differently.

Baptized on my fortieth birthday, we held a big bash at the ranch. I'd been sober for ninety days and my parents and old friends came to celebrate, along with my new friends at the ranch. That night when I returned home, a series of circumstances surrounding my family came crashing toward me like a tsunami wave. I automatically started to respond out of my old pattern of dealing with pain and trauma. Desperately, I *longed* for a drink to hide the fear I was feeling.

Making the difficult choice to pick up the phone rather than give into alcohol, I dialed Teresa's number. She heard fear in my voice and immediately urged, "Debra, come stay with us until the craving passes. We'll help you." The day we met, Teresa had promised to help. Now in my hour of personal crisis, she was following through so I could stay sober.

From that point, something changed profoundly. When I made the choice to reach out and receive help in a time of dire straits, alcohol lost its grip. The obsession and compulsion to drink left, and has never returned.

Part Of The Body
Now, I'm part of New Hope Christian Fellowship, the church that meets at the ranch. My new Christian friends have shown me I cannot make it *alone*. We need each other for growth, counsel and accountability, always pointing each other back to Jesus with the utmost truthful love.

I've begun to know who I am. No longer passive and powerless like a 'doormat', I've learned to set personal boundaries and to value and honor myself, just as Jesus instructs us to *love our neighbor as we **love ourselves**.*[38] As an intercessor in

---

[38] *Mark 12:31*

the body of Christ, I've also found a place of spiritual fulfill-ment that constantly brings me back to seeking Jesus first, family second and putting everything else in third place.

My daughter, Halsey, has come through her own battle with alcohol and now as a young Mom, is walking well with Jesus as her Savior and Friend. Gem, my youngest child, is a happy elementary school-aged powerhouse. Together, we're all changing and growing.

Trusting others, trusting God and learning to express frustra-tion and other negative emotions instead of holding them in: these are some of the fruits of my own healing and personal discipline. I'm letting people into my life to love me uncondi-tionally and now, when I need help, I tell people. Rigorous honesty has become a part of relational love that makes us all flourish vibrantly.

Before Christ, I couldn't have dreamed of speaking in front of anyone: now, I am filled with His boldness. Before knowing Jesus, I avoided 'messy' people: now, He loves them through me and I walk *toward* them, rather than away. And when I don't feel like doing something I know I'm supposed to do, I choose to do it anyway!

I'm learning to lay down my life, praying for others as people once prayed for me in my times of need. Focusing on Jesus, I receive His love and minister to others around me, as He points out their need. Together we serve and make a differ-ence, one life at a time.

7

JOURNEYING WITH GOD

Cleansing Love

Teresa and I are examples of how lifelong journeys with God might play out for those coming out of a world system. We arrived in the kingdom of God as broken, deceived individuals and God took the turns and twists of our past and started pouring in the Holy Spirit, His Living Water. He purified and cleansed our lives, washing away everything that was stagnant, putrid and polluted.

When we began our journeys as newly recovering alcoholics, we only had a tiny wisp of hope that we could someday lead a ministry to help others find recovery. And certainly at that time, the possibilities of pastoring a church, training and equipping believers, and walking in healing evangelism - all ministries that we're currently carrying out - were ideas we'd not even begun to consider. In those early days, we only knew we needed help and we needed *love.*

The healing and growth we all require as new believers can be aborted if we try to rush God's processes. That's one reason God, in His wisdom, only uncovers each step of our life when the time is right for its revealing. He may give us prophetic words to provide hope and vision for the future, but actual specifics like where to go and what to do, often only fall into place as we need to know the next direction to take.

Taking Teresa and me from brokenness to wholeness, from spiritual illegitimacy to adoption as His children, we had to first experience His Fatherhood and the tenderness of His Holy Spirit. He took the time required to *Father us* back into His affection, using people to demonstrate His love and guide us in maturation. He nurtured us during each season of growth until we could embrace the next chapter of what He'd been holding in trust.

God's Mysterious Guidance

All humans want to know their destiny: we all want to figure out *who we are* and to feel like we've *fulfilled our purpose* on this big ball called earth. Human beings feel a sense of significance when we discover what makes us 'tick'. Ultimately, we won't be satisfied unless we know why God created us.

So, God speaks to us, through the Bible *and* in other ways, to reveal His good plans for our lives. Prophetic words are one kind of personal, heavenly message to help focus our lives and reveal *our identity* from heaven's perspective. For example, I have received quite a few prophetic words that confirmed evangelism as one of numerous spiritual gifts in my life. These prophecies were a signpost from the Trinity, who created me, and knows me infinitely better than anyone else. God used prophetic words to clue me in on this aspect of my identity, so I could then seek further direction in how to grow in my gift as an evangelist.

God uses many different things to show us the pathway toward our fulfillment. The desires in our hearts, prophetic words, circumstances and the encouragement of others, all help us see His purposes. He also uses *dreams* and *visions*. All of these supernatural languages of the Spirit come alongside the Word of God to help direct and shape our lives. They're a gift from heaven to be prayed over, and it's a good idea to also share them with other believers for testing and discernment.

We mention here the ways God communicates, because they are an essential part of how He makes His plans known. The scope of this writing is not to teach how the Spirit speaks: many books have already been written on that subject and we encourage you to pursue reading them, for more understanding on God's forms of communication. Several sources we have found helpful are listed at the end of this book in the *Recommended Reading* section.

The Unveiling of Gifts

The *timings* of heaven are also important to consider. I've mentioned in previous chapters that God moves a lot more slowly than I often think He should! Teresa and I both carried plans and desires in our hearts for years before they actually came to pass. Prophetic words or dreams can be released five, ten or even twenty years before their fulfillment so that while we're being healed and matured, we will have hope. He knows, in order to embrace the future with expectation of His goodness and to keep our hopes and dreams alive, we need promises to walk by in every period of change.

> *He knows we need promises to walk by, in every period of change*

Early on in our spiritual journeys, while growing as a son and daughter of God, our heavenly Father gradually unveiled to Teresa and me our spiritual gifts. The first time I had an inkling that I was good at sharing my faith publicly was during the early days of my own recovery from alcohol. Standing in Alcoholics Anonymous meetings and excitedly giving a testimony about something God had done in my life, I would sense God's presence beginning to touch people in the room. I had no clue then, that speaking was part of my spiritual DNA: that understanding would come later in my journey.

Years later, Rob Bagley sat down beside me at a weekly pastors' gathering. Rob is a pastor with a strong prophetic gifting and as he leaned into our conversation he observed, "Rick, every time we're in one of these meetings, you always turn the discussion around to finding the lost. Everyone else is talking about some function of their church, and you want to turn it into an outreach." As I processed Rob's words, God confirmed one of my gifts was evangelism.

Primarily, I'm happiest when I can share Him with others, especially the broken and captive. That's one reason I also have been given a gift of healing. God wants people to know His power to meet their needs.

With this renewed understanding about my personal gifts, God then placed me in situation after situation, to build confidence and affirm His gifts within. We were invited to be part of the leadership team for a series of *outpouring meetings* in the city of Reno. Still lacking confidence, in part because we simply hadn't had a lot of experience in praying for healings on a larger scale, Teresa and I stepped out anyway and God met us with His miracle-working power.

One woman there had a mangled and deformed foot. We prayed for her and God began to touch her heart. At the end of the night she approached us and was bubbling over with excitement. Except for a callous that had formed because of walking crooked, she'd been healed. Her foot had completely straightened out and she was able to walk normally!

Teresa ministered to another woman in a wheelchair who couldn't walk at all. After a few minutes of prayer, Teresa sensed by the Holy Spirit there was faith for the woman to stand up. She turn and said boldly, "It's time to act on faith: stand up!" Getting up out of her wheelchair, the woman was able to walk for the first time in years. She received her healing that night!

God used the miracles and healings at the outpouring to train us and build our faith, teaching us our authority in Him. As He gave us 'words of knowledge' we called them out and saw deliverances from addictions, emotional healings and lots of physical healings.[39] Added to what we'd already seen at the ranch - diseases leaving the men in the program, people being healed in our church, a blind goat receiving sight (and the goat's eye color changing from blue to brown!), a baby pig coming back to life, horses being healed, a sterile cow birthing a calf, and more - our understanding of who *we are in Jesus* and who *He is in us,* grew in leaps and bounds.

Later, we held three months of revival tent meetings at the Ranch. Joe Cicchino[40] led the gatherings and Teresa and I facilitated. Seeing God meet so many needs during these meetings continued to increase our faith. Many people were healed and delivered from demonic oppression. Perhaps our favorite testimony from that time was when a hearing impaired couple was able to communicate using sound for the first time in their marriage. They had never before heard each other's voices until their hearing was restored that night!

Up And Out

Someone has said 'God always trades up', meaning, as we grow in Him and yield more of our lives, our surrender is met with much more of His goodness than we could have envi-

---

[39] *1 Corinthians 12:8-11*

[40] For more on Joe's ministry: www.visionoflove.org

sioned. Since the early days of returning to God, the borders of what Teresa and I have been given to steward have continued to expand. This increase is only natural in the kingdom, because the King loves to bless.

Outside of Christ we lived dead lives, in a downward spiral of lack. But *in* Christ we live upward and outward. Isaiah speaks of this reality, instructing those who have been 'won over' by God, to prepare for expansion:

> "Enlarge the place of your tent, stretch your tent curtains wide, do not hold back; lengthen your cords, strengthen your stakes. For you will spread out to the right and to the left; your descendants will dispossess nations and settle in their desolate cities."
>
> Isaiah 54:2,3 *NIV*

In the context of this passage, those who are told to prepare for expansion are the 'barren': the empty-handed. It is their descendants who dispossess the enemy's territory. Those whose lives were empty before meeting Christ, *expand* when they are in Jesus.

Multiplication

When God wants to establish a new work, He orchestrates His plan by first *revealing a need.* Then, He *moves people into position* to meet the need. Several needs have recently become apparent to us and we're cooperating with the Holy Spirit's nudges in our hearts to be ones who respond.

137

A few years ago, we realized another personal shift was coming and we began preparing to hand oversight of New Hope's Recovery Ranch to several excellent leaders. Pastors Rodney and Bonnie Williams are now directing New Hope's daily operations, with pastor Randy Cook contributing greatly to the spiritual mentoring of the men.

For a while, New Hope has housed only men at the ranch since, for various reasons, we sensed we needed to close down ministering to both men and women at the same facility. Shortly after we handed leadership of the men's ranch over to the Williams, Teresa was barraged with women who were desperate for the same opportunity of freedom that New Hope currently provides as a 'men only' facility.

> *When God wants to establish a new work, He orchestrates His plan by first revealing a need.*

After prayerful discernment, we sensed that God was directing us to establish another addictions recovery home, separate from New Hope's men's facility, and just for women. A women's home fits very well with Teresa's gifts for counseling and mentoring women. As a result, we have recently opened the *New Hope Kimberly Lee House* for women, in honor of my daughter.

At the beginning of last year Kim died of complications stemming from her battle with alcoholism. Now that you know something about our personal journeys, you probably understand that God's *protection* and *blessing* in the life of a believer look more like being taken safely *through* 'valleys of the shadow of death', rather than skirting them entirely and escaping all difficulties.[41] God promises to guide us with His rod and staff: He gives support and direction as well as deliverance, but we still have to walk through challenges to get to victory on the other side.

That has been the case with our own families. Our salvations and baptisms of the Holy Spirit began processes of reconciliation with members of our family who had been hurt by our alcoholism. Sadly, both Teresa's sister and my daughter Kim ended up walking the same pathway of dependency on alcohol that we once lived, and both died from complications related to alcohol.

For years, Kim and I were estranged. We had only recently begun the process of opening up communication together, when she died. I would have liked to see her freed from alcohol and I certainly wanted more time to heal my relationship with her, but we choose to trust God. His justice is so much higher than our earthly viewpoint. He hates when we're robbed and in His mercy, God will do what is right and best. Isaiah 61:8 *NIV*, makes this promise to us: *"For I, the Lord, love justice; I hate robbery and iniquity. In my faithfulness I will reward (my people) and make an everlasting covenant with them."*

In one way, our new women's facility is a form of divine justice. Women who have been trapped by the same alcohol abuse that consumed Kim will be brought into healing and

---

[41] *Psalm 23*

deliverance. Multiplied seeds of life will come out of our personal loss.

Like The Wind

Jesus compared those who are 'born of the Spirit' to the invisible movement of the wind: you can hear it, but you can't tell where it's going.[42] This Scripture has certainly been true in our lives. As we've endeavored to follow God, always adjusting to His direction, He's made life a tremendous adventure!

In this increasingly fast-paced society with fluctuating economic trends, widespread travel possibilities and instantaneous worldwide internet communication, we need to stay flexible and embrace new things. We don't fear: we're not going to 'shrink back', even when we don't understand difficulties that come our way.[43] Instead, we move ahead in the power of the Holy Spirit, the love of the Father and the authority of the Lord Jesus, trusting our Heavenly Family, the Trinity. They invite us to walk with them as their healed and confident sons and daughters of God, bringing the kingdom of God from heaven to earth and making disciples wherever we go.

---

[42] *John 3:8*
[43] *Hebrews 10:39*

For Further Reflection

1. There are three passages in the Bible where specific spiritual gifts are listed: 1 Corinthians 12; Ephesians 4:4-16; Romans 12:1-10. Read these passages and ask God to 'identify' you and point out the gifts He's placed into your life. Also, ask wise friends and mature mentors for their observations about your strengths and weaknesses. Even our weaknesses can help identify our gifts, by eliminating what doesn't 'fit' our personality. Continue to seek God for direction in identifying you: in the coming weeks, watch Him give you 'clues' about yourself and how He made you.

2. Where has God been working to build your confidence? Read about Joshua's preparation and how God calls him to courage in Exodus 24:13, Deuteronomy 3:28 and Joshua 1:1-9. How do you think being mentored by Moses, and being in God's presence on the mountain and in the 'tent of meeting' made a difference in Joshua's ability to fulfill his call? In chapter one of the book of Joshua, what practical advice did God emphasize for Joshua's strengthening? Ask God how you could apply those same things for your own encouragement.

3. Do you have a sense of where you are in the processes of God for your life? Is this a season of rest and refreshment for

you? Of healing, nurture and receiving more of His love? Of growing in gifts? Of stepping out into new ventures? Understanding where we are in the process of growth with God, helps us see what He's currently working into our hearts and gives grace to fully embrace what He's doing. Ask God to reveal His ways for your life and share with a trusted believer what you're sensing.

Prayer:

Father, You are good. Thank You for walking with me. Show me Your ways for my life and lead me into Your purposes. Give me patience to trust that Your timings for my life are perfect, and help me fully know my identity as Your child. Give me courage and boldness to 'be all you made me to be'. Above all, draw me closer to You and let me feel Your presence in and through my everyday activities. I love You.

Jeff Cline's Gift Of Life

More than anything in life, I was driven to chase after pleasure. Drugs, illicit sexual rendezvous with women and most of all alcohol, topped my list of favorite indulgences. As a married man striking out on sexual trysts, alcohol provided the fuel needed to dull my moral convictions so I could freely engage in adultery and stimulating drug usage.

Living a secret life forced me to become an excellent liar, and my deceits took on many different forms as I tried to hide my habit. Turning my head during conversations so people couldn't smell alcohol on my breath or notice the bloodshot whites of my eyes, I used Listerine, breath mints, peanut butter and even onions, to cover up the scent of constantly drinking booze. When I lied to my wife, friends, co-workers or anyone else, I never looked them in the eye. Learning to think ahead, I worked hard to remember which lie I told in certain locations or to certain people, in order to collaborate reality with deception.

As an alcoholic who continued to drink and drive, I also tried very hard to outsmart the police. Constantly on the lookout for squad cars, I trained myself not to take a swallow of alcohol while driving through intersections and I always made certain to come to a complete stop at crossroads. I often drove while partially or fully inebriated, but in the foolish reasoning of my alcoholic fog, I figured I'd be all right if I was careful. Getting behind the steering wheel of a car was a life-threatening risk I was willing to take in order to feed my passions. When my stupidity landed me in court and I was served two counts of 'Driving Under The Influence', I began to wake up to the reality that I had to change, and checked myself into the program at *New Hope Recovery Ranch*. But without alcohol's numbing of mind or morals, I hated me and was terrified to face the man I'd become. Full of *anger*, I exploded at Rick, Teresa and the other program participants whenever they crossed my path. I felt completely and utterly unlovable. But the McKinneys demonstrated patience and honor in spite of my anger. Slowly, they gave me small tastes of Father God's love for prodigal sons.[44] Over time, their love and the love of God broke through my self-hatred to enable the slow process of healing and recovery.

Eight years later, at age fifty-two, I'm a new man. Thankfully, my wonderful wife was willing to stay with me and endure the years of my deceitfulness and addiction, until I finally arrived at sobriety. This year, we will celebrate twenty-eight years of marriage. How incredibly grateful I am that God did not give up on me! Neither did my wife and a few faithful friends. All of my life I owe to God's grace and to true believers who were willing to give their lives to bring one deceived drunkard into the grace of sobering Truth. These are the greatest gifts of my life.

---

[44] *Luke 15:20*

Acknowledgments

First and foremost I want to thank Father God, the Lord Jesus Christ and the Holy Spirit for never leaving me or forsaking me, even in my deepest times of trial, and for bringing me into the place of relationship with Them. Second, I would like to thank my wife Teresa for supporting this ministry and me. At the beginning, she tolerated thirteen men at a time living in our house, bless her heart! She has been a wonderful wife and a great partner in the work the Lord has given us to do. Honey, I thank you with all my heart!

I would also like to attempt to acknowledge the other people who have participated and poured into our lives and ministries, though it is impossible for me to remember every single person who has given and blessed. I would like to thank Mom and Dad for standing by me when I was using drugs and drinking and not following the Lord. They were angry and hurt, yet never abandoned me. Though they are home with the Lord now, my appreciation of all the things they poured into me has only continued to grow.

Thank you, Richard P., for being at Peralta Hospital in Oakland, Ca., when I arrived there slightly intoxicated and without hope. As four men carried me up the stairs to the detoxification unit, I remember the words you spoke to me: " Rick, you never have to do this again". Thank you for those words of hope, Richard, and for all the hours you spent counseling me. Thank you, Bob and Lee Kozlowski, for the inspiration and counseling you did with me in my early recovery. Thanks for teaching me how to ride a horse while I cried to you about my circumstances. Animals now play a large part in our program, since we use the same model of healing through animal 'therapy', here at the ranch. Many men have been helped with the same principles you used for my own healing.

Thank you to Pastors Darrell and Gwen Cluck for putting up with me before I came to the realization of Christ in my life. I'd go to church drunk and Darrell would acknowledge me without embarrassing me. In 1980 - when I couldn't live *or* die - I walked into his Pentecostal Holiness church and recommitted my life to Christ. I want to thank him for his persistence in counseling me about the Holy Spirit and leading me in the baptism of the Holy Spirit. He taught me about the gifts of the Holy Spirit as well as the principals of God. Thank you for starting that strong foundation in my life.

Thank you to Dr. Robert Schuller: I told the Lord that it would be awesome if one day I could meet Robert Schuller and

Acknowledgments

thank him for his broadcasts about positive thinking, and God arranged that encounter on the patio of the Crystal Cathedral. Dr, Schuller prayed for our vision of the ministry of *New Hope Recovery Ranch* and for provision and even more vision. Thank you, Dr. Schuller.

A special thank you to my precious sister-in-law Peggy Leavitt, for catching the vision and being willing to help us out. Thank you for donating the money for the down payment on the ranch and for your love and support for our ministry, and just being a part of our lives. I know you are home with Jesus now and I believe in my heart that when you saw Jesus, you did what I requested and told Him *I am doing the best I can* and that we love Him. You have our eternal love, Peggy.

A special thank you to Manette, my other precious sister-in-law for her love and support too. Thank you to my brothers Vern, George and my sister Karen, for their love through my darker days and their many prayers. Thank you to my cousin, Steve Turner, a mighty man of God and a blazing missionary! Thank you for your zeal, your prophetic anointing and your never-failing words of encouragement, not to mention your help with the church and the ranch. Steve, we love you. Thank you to my son Gary, for his continued love and support in spite of growing up in the shadow of my fathering mistakes. Thank you Gary, for letting the Holy Spirit fill you and for your love for Jesus Christ and Father God. Thank you to Veronica my precious daughter-in-law, a rich blessing in our lives, healed of cancer by Jesus. Thank you to my special little granddaughter, Desi: my little cowgirl who can ride any horse we can put under her and who loves her grandpa very much. Thank you Des, for your love.

Thank you to my beautiful and sweet little girl Kimberly Lee, for teaching me something about humility, unconditional love and hope. I know, Kimmie, that you're dancing with the angels in heaven and I know that you know how much Daddy really loves you. I WILL see you again and dance with you. Thank you to all the rest of my kids and grandkids too: - Tanya, Matt and Nick, Beth, David, Megan, Jason and Owen, Ben and Kaila - for all of your love and prayers.

Thank you to Maureen for your love and support for the ministry and I know that the Lord has blessed you and will continue to bless you for this. Thank you for the hours that you spent ministering to my precious wife and sponsoring her through her early days of sobriety. Your insight and wisdom has made our lives richer.

Thank you to Pastor Kay Peterson for her love and prophetic insight into NHRR and our ministry. She's the one who reminded me that 'even Peter had to get out of the boat and walk on water', a perfect word in season. She also introduced us to Joe and Betty Ferguson. Thank you Joe, for your love and your insight that confirms Proverbs 27:17, that 'iron sharpens iron'. Kay also introduced us to Bob and Molly Smith who poured much into our ministry. Bob is home with Jesus now and I miss him dearly, but we still have Mama Molly who is on our board today and we love her dearly and cherish her words of wisdom. Bob was instrumental in teaching me about raising cows, goats and ranch life in general, and also introduced me to Aaron and Donelle Williams, who have blessed this ministry beyond measure. Aaron and Donelle, you have such great wisdom beyond your years. Thank you for your insight and for teaching me and working with me in raising cattle. Thank you Aaron for donating our first 5 pregnant heifers and one awesome Beefmaster bull (the boys named him Arnold-for Arnold Schwarzenegger). Thank you for allowing the men in the program to be a part of your ranch too, for letting them come over and brand and vaccinate cattle and participate with other true Christian cowboys. I love you very much.

Thank you to Pastors Matt and Regina McCreary for pastoring us, and to Living Faith Christian Fellowship for supporting our ministry for such a long time. I love you both, you truly are a brother and a sister to Teresa and me.

Thank you to Pastor Dallas Ramsey for taking Teresa and me under your wing and introducing us to other people with similar visions like ours, for sending us the men from the mission that needed more time. Most of all, thanks for being our friend and for your unconditional love. We love you, Dallas. Thank you to Pastors Tom Chism and Jim Bedmark from Yerington Vineyard Fellowship, for your love, support and counseling. God bless you both. Thank you to Sparks Christian Fellowship for your love and continued support of our ministry.

Thank you to Ted Bigley for teaching us about the Father's heart, and about deliverance and spiritual gifts: for allowing us to be part of your ministry and to learn and glean from you. We love you and Ginger very much. Thank you to David Smith for the prophetic words you have given me and for your love and guidance. I remember when you and Todd Bentley prophesied over me at BMF Camp in the Sierras, that I was to 'move into ministry and do it quickly'. Thank you for your friendship and support. We love you and your beautiful wife, Renee (my favorite), and the kids. Our prayer is that the Lord will continue to bless American Engineering in Rocklin, Ca., as you have blessed us. We love you, David.

Thank you to Al and Sue Kuhn: two very special people the Lord strategically planted in our lives and ministry. I especially want to thank you for allowing God to guide you in purchasing the ranch across the road from our property, originally for use as a women's recovery home and now for a meeting place for our church, New Hope Christian Fellowship. You and Sue have been wonderful friends and such a blessing to us. Thank you for the special ministry trips to Pasadena, where we were able to meet Che Ahn and be part of a fantastic praise and worship symposium. Thank you for letting Teresa and I use your cabin in the 'secret place' to get away once in awhile to seek the Lord, or to just relax and have fun. We bless and honor you very much and we love you. We know that we will continue to minister together for a long time. We pray blessings on your project, *Big Al's BBQ*, an evangelistic, spirit-filled, good tasting, great atmospheric experience. We love you two!

A very special thank you to Virgil Langson, who at this time is 93 years young! Thank you for being one of my spiritual fathers. I never will forget the day we met at Sierra Men's camp and talked about our dear friend, Bob Smith, who had already gone home to Jesus. There was an instant bonding between the two of us. I want to thank you for your spiritual and financial faithfulness over the last decade. Love you, Ole' Virg, and sweet Lucy, and see you soon.

Acknowledgments

Thank you to Bob and Michele Wright for being so faithful to the ministry. Michele, it has been such an awesome experience for us to watch you as you go to different countries and spread the gospel, heal the sick and open blind eyes. Bob and Michele, thank you too, for your friendship and all the good memories we have had together. We look forward to many more. You truly are a brother and a sister to Teresa and me.

Thank you to my sister, Linda Langley, for giving me constructive tips about my preaching apparel (not to wear white tennis shoes). That was very important to me. Thank you for filming those little documentaries about the ranch; they truly helped to explain our purpose here. Thank you to James and Diane Barham for all of the fun and refreshing get-away times: for sitting at your feet, James, and listening to your exploits with Jesus and for your great hospitality, Diane. We love you guys and cherish our friendship. A special thanks to John and Joyce Gavin, of Dayton, NV, for your friendship, your advice and your support. You truly are a good man, John Gavin, and you have a very sweet wife!

Thank you for our special team at the ranch and the church that God has brought together. Pastors Scott and LaDonna Vollmer, Pastor Randy Cook, and Pastors Rodney and Bonnie Williams: we love and appreciate each one of you for your special gifts and friendships. What an awesome group to work with; thank you! Scott and LaDonna, thank you for being a part of our ministry almost from the start. Your support, insight, advice and love have truly helped to guide us. Thank you, too, for being such good friends! Thank you, Scott, for your willingness to preach, teach and prophesy at a moment's notice! Thank you! LaDonna, you have been such a wonderful help to the ministry and like a sister to me. I appreciate your Spirit-filled teaching of our young people and your prophetic gifts you have imparted to them. It is fun to watch them prophesy, lay hands on the sick and testify of God's goodness. Thank you for working at the food bank and all that entails! Awesome! Love you, LaDonna.

Randy, thank you for your help, your obedience, your advice and your unique personality. You have been with us for ten years and it has been fun. Thank you for your undying support and enthusiasm in working with the men in the program. I know you have been a great inspiration to each one. We very much appreciate your teaching anointing at the ranch and the church. It has been wonderful to watch you grow all these years, beginning when you came into the program to get sober and to get God in your life. You truly are one of God's favorites and our favorite as well! We love you.

Rodney and Bonnie, thank you two for what you've done out at the ranch with the men and the church. It truly is a pleasure to be able to work so closely with you. You are doing a fantastic job! Rodney, it's awesome to see how God is increasing your spiritual gifts, your preaching and your discipling of the men. Bonnie, thank you for all your awesome work in the office and your support for all of us and for your prayers. We need them! We love you guys and your whole family!

A very big thank you to Terry and Cheryl Edwards for their apostolic role in our lives and our ministry. It truly is an honor, Terry and Cheryl, to be under your spiritual covering and to be a small part of your ministry at Lake Tahoe Christian Fellowship. Thank you also for your friendship and your love and your encouragement in all that God has called us to do. We look forward to many more years of experiences and fellowship together. Thank you for taking us on our first out-of-country ministry trip to the Philippines. Terry, you have done an awesome work in putting together all of those apostolic leaders and ministers in so many churches in the Philippines. It was very much an honor to be able to minister with you and see so many deliverances and healings, baptisms in the Holy Spirit and salvations. Thank you Terry and thank you Cheryl, for supporting your husband in the many projects he takes on. You're an awesome sister.

And last but certainly not least, thank you to Janet and Rusty for taking on the vision to write this book for us. When we first met at Bethel and you said you would pray about writing this book, we had no idea how many hours, prayers and probably even tears that this would require. You guys are the best and we love you and thank you so much for writing our story for all to read. Our prayer is that God would be glorified in all that we do or say in our lives. Thank you, thank you, thank you and looking forward to the next one! God bless you and love you guys!

We promise that the *acknowledgments* will not be this long in the next book! We tried not to forget anyone but we probably have, since we are only human. So, forgive us if we did, and we will catch you on the next go around.

Recommended Reading

Good Morning, Holy Spirit, Benny Hinn*[45]

When Heaven Invades Earth, Bill Johnson

Face to Face with God, Bill Johnson

The Supernatural Ways of Royalty, Kris Vallotton

Seed Faith, Oral Roberts

Don't Park Here, Oral Roberts

Daughter of Destiny (Bio of Kathryn Kuhlman), Jamie Buckingham

The Triumphant Church, Kenneth Hagin

Growing in the Prophetic, Mike Bickel*

The Seer, Jim Goll*

Supernatural: The life of William Branham: Volumes 1-4,
    Owen Jorgensen

---

[45] **Titles with an asterisk are specifically recommended for growth in hearing God prophetically (as referred to in chapter 7)*

Appendix A
Mashach Ministries, Inc.

Sent Ones

The biblical word for mentoring and helping mature another Christ-follower, is *discipling*. Jesus tells His followers to 'go and make *disciples* of all *nations*', or *ethnos*, as the Greek language translates the word *nation*.[46] Simply stated, Jesus is telling us to introduce Him to all the cultural peoples of the earth, and to mature those who want to be His friends.

That's where *Mashach Ministries* comes into the picture. *Mashach* means *anoint* in the Hebrew language. God has given Teresa and me gifts of preaching, healing, evangelism, counsel and deliverance. Partnering with the anointing of the Spirit, we want to release these gifts for the sake of both *believers* and *'pre-Christians'* out there in the world.

The New Testament apostles were *sent out*.[47] We are also sent out, bringing a two-fold ministry approach of *evangelism* to unbelievers, and *equipping* for the saints. Similar to the ministry of Paul the apostle as he related to the early churches, we

---

[46] *Matthew 28:19, NIV*
[47] *'sent ones' is the basic biblical meaning of the word* apostle

preach and release healing, deliverance and ministry to the 'unchurched' at *outreach gatherings* in a city or town. Alongside outreach gatherings, we also offer *smaller meetings for believers* at area churches. Working with pastors and leaders, our call is to help *equip* their people in various aspects of Spirit-empowered evangelism, deliverance and healing. We also offer addictions recovery ministry by leading and/or training others to lead weekly twelve-step gatherings like the model we've used at our recovery ranch.

Some practical training sessions we offer for equipping include, but are not limited to: *Twelve Spirit-Filled Steps to Freedom from Addiction, How to Pray for Physical Healing, The Baptism of the Holy Spirit, Deliverance as a Key Toward Victory* and *Principles of Growing With God.*

This two-fold approach of *evangelism outreach* and *discipleship training* enables believers in every local expression of the body of Christ to walk in greater maturity, while also reaching out to bring freedom to the lost.

If you are interested in knowing more about Mashach Ministries, Inc., please contact us at:

Mashach Ministries, Inc.
Pastors Rick and Teresa McKinney
PO Box 961
Silver Springs, NV 89429
Email: newhoperr1@aol.com
Website: www.newhope-church.com

Appendix B

The Twelve Steps And Spiritual Disciplines[48]

Recognizing our brokenness

1. We admitted we were powerless over the effects of our separation from God - that our lives had become unmanageable.

> *Romans 7:17:* I know nothing good lives in me, that is, my sinful nature. For I have the desire to do what is good, but I cannot carry it out.

The birth of faith in us

2. Came to believe that a power greater than ourselves could restore us to sanity.

> *Philippians 2:13:* For it is God who works in you to will and to act according to his good purpose.

A decision to let God be in charge of our lives.

---

[48] *Copyright information on The Twelve Steps and Spiritual Disciplines is listed at the front of the book.*

3. Made a decision to turn our will and our lives over to the care of God as we understood Him.

> *Romans 1:21* Therefore, I urge you, brothers, in view of God's mercy, to offer your bodies as living sacrifices, holy and pleasing to God - which is your spiritual worship.

Self examination

4. Made a searching and fearless moral inventory of ourselves.

> *Lamentations 3:40* Let us examine our ways and test them, and let us return to the Lord.

The discipline of confession.

5. Admitted to God, to ourselves, and to another human being the exact nature of our wrongs.

> *James 5:16a* Therefore, confess your sins to each other and pray for each other so that you may be healed.

An inner transformation sometimes called repentance.

6. Were entirely ready to have God remove all these defects of character.

> *James 4:10* Humble yourselves before the Lord and He will lift you up.

The transformation or purification of our character.

7. Humbly asked Him to remove our shortcomings.

1 John 1:9 If we confess our sins, He is faithful and just and will forgive us our sins and purify us from all unrighteousness.

Examining our relationships and preparing ourselves to make amends.

8. Made a list of all persons we had harmed and became willing to make amends to them all.

Luke 6:31 Do unto others as you would have them do to you.

The discipline of making amends.

9. Made direct amends to such people wherever possible, except when to do so would injure them or others.

Matthew 5:23,24 Therefore, if you are offering your gift at the altar and there remember that your brother has something against you, leave your gift there in front of the altar. First go and be reconciled to your brother; then come and offer your gift.

Maintaining progress in recovery.

10. Continued to take personal inventory and when we were wrong, promptly admitted it.

> *1 Corinthians 10:12* So, if you think you are standing firm, be careful that you don't fall.

The spiritual disciplines of prayer and meditation.

11. Sought through prayer and meditation to improve our conscious contact with God, as we understood Him, praying only for knowledge of His will for us and the power to carry that out.

> *Colossians 3:16a* Let the word of Christ dwell in you richly.

Ministry.

12. Having had a spiritual awakening as the result of these Steps, we tried to carry this message to others, and to practice these principles in all our affairs.

> *Galatians 6:1* Brothers, if someone is caught in a sin, you who are spiritual should restore him gently. But watch yourself, or you may also be tempted.